ALBION STREET POEMS & SHORT STORIES

K McVere

Albion Street Poems & Short Stories. Copyright © 2020 by K McVere. All rights reserved. Printed in the United States of America. No part of this publication may be reproduced, distributed, or transmitted in any form or by any means, including photocopying, recording, digital scanning, or other electronic or mechanical methods without the prior written permission of the publisher, except in the case of brief quotations embodied in critical reviews and certain other noncommercial uses permitted by copyright law. Any queries or permission requests address to K McVere LLC.

K McVere LLC.
P.O. Box 50262
Boise, ID 83705

ISBN: 978-0-578-58099-9

Cover design by Red Couch Creative, inc.
Interior design by K McVere LLC

Department of English, Boise State University, *cold-drill magazine:*
Kelley J. Miller contributor

Wedged Between		1999
Reunion at Saint Croix		1999
40 Watts		1999
Making an Impression		2000
Them Cockeyed Optimists	kmcvere.wordpress.com	2019

The poetry is autobiographical and subject to personal experience wherein names have been changed and some events fictionalized. All characters and events in the short story collection are fictitious. Any resemblance to persons living or dead is strictly coincidental.

CONTENTS

POEMS

WEDGED BETWEEN

The graveled road soothes him
with fields of cut wheat and mint, an
audience of cows and sunset sky.
beneath his feet, the earth whispers,
turning beds of lava, granite and sand.

Owyhee waits, orphaned in burned meadows
and raw burrows, sleeping in blankets
of sagebrush, thistle and thorn, nose
tipped to kiss the phantom moon, lulled by
the song of crickets.

And he listens, rubbing a stone
between cold fingers, pulling back from
concrete and glass, sirens wailing,
and fanged shiny metal shooting into the sky—
now wedged, between daydreams and firelight.

Wees Bar waits, while arrow heads nest
in fields beside the Snake River,
alongside humped backs of Walrus rock,
lost messages from Shoshone and Blackfoot—
now voices asleep, in canyon winds and sage beds.

And he listens, to anything metal,
of moving parts, birthed by rubber, chrome, exhaust,
all that is speed pulls at him, and yet
in the firelight, his rough chapped hands,
polish stone, engraving messages to those who wait.

REUNION AT ST. CROIX

This moment, I will remember this moment forever.
Along the banks of the St. Croix river,
eating tuna sandwiches, sipping bottled water,
sitting on the sandy shore, wet bathing suits drying,
we watch canoes drift by.

Wispy clouds float overhead, their reflections
drifting in clear water. As green dragonfly
darts along waves, a miniature helicopter,
pausing to hover over orange safety jackets,
its body suspended in air by the art of its wings.

Tiny gnats buzz around our feet. The sun warms our backs
and glitters on lapping water. In the woods behind us,
birds quarrel and squirrels curse us from tree limbs.
The smell of fish, seaweed, sand and suntan lotion
drifts through our pores and settles in our lungs.

I rest my chin on my knee, safe. For this moment.

40 WATTS

Alone with me, a note pad and pencil
at her side, a scribbled message
I must decipher while hot blue eyes
examine a rare specimen between glass, I say
"You want to watch something on TV?"

Right side frowns left side quivers up.
Before images winking, our hands are
soft curves, our bodies stiff in quiet rooms.
No one crying, shouting, or arguing,
just silence between heartbeats.

Her fingers: skins of crisp, dry sticks,
meet mine in templed wetness.
Once they flew over typewriter keys,
flipped pages in a book, spanked bare
bottoms, and combed knots into silk.

Alone with me, tiled walls dance,
my blood drained fingers wriggle, while
mini blinds snap to the music of cold,
artificial air. Beyond this, there might be a sun
or a 40-watt bulb burning in a smoked-filled room.

MY FIVE FATHERS

I can count them on one hand.
They were never a bushel or a peck.
More a flyspeck. With one exception.

And when Momma dusts them off, we are five:
Momma, me, middle girl, youngest girl,
youngest only boy. We are then prime.
Prime is special. Prime is good.

My five fathers make the family even.
Not special. Not prime.
Between fathers we were special, we were good.
With fathers, not so good. With one exception.

Am I grateful? On good days.
On good days, I can agree,
I can agree I learned so much from my five fathers.
Thank you, dear fathers. Let me count the ways.

My first father taught me to tie my shoes,
and wait for him and wonder where he'd gone.

My second father taught me to fear the belt,
and hate baked beans and love train travel.

My third father taught me the Civil War never ended
and how much this Yankee girl couldn't wait to get home.

My fourth father wasn't around long enough to teach me
anything. He was a pit stop on Mamma's way to her final
and special destination.

Today,
my fifth father, he, the last of my five fathers,
he teaches me

– how to love my mother.

ROLLING-PIN WARRIOR

On a cold September dawn, she was
the one we dressed for, upon the thorny grass,
in front of his house, our soles pricked
by puncture weeds.

We clung to each other,
fumbling in bags, fingers trembling along seams,
along cotton shorts. Me, I ran ahead, anxious
to be gone, hearing, "Stop, Stop. Wait for us." I wait.
Defeated. Sure, he'll catch us. But no. Luck. Pure Luck
saved us. We got away; Scott Free.

She loved him once, he, a familiar cruelty. Not me.
I hated him, the instructor grading my punching of pillows,
my tucks and snappy corners with welts and furious silences,
his instructions never forgotten. Even today, my bed is always
made before breakfast, an education born from terror.

We became Scott Free, not for childhood welts and sideways
slaps, but for a last straw, a morning wakeup call, a gun
to the head, a vow to kill her if she ever left him. A lesson
for me: ignore the welts, the choking, the cries - save yourself.

One day she proved me wrong. With a rolling pin,
she, the avenger, beat a Jack down the stairs, a Queen
Boudica shouting "Out, Out, Out!" arm raised, striking –
once, twice, and a third time. The cracks satisfactory,
hardwood sounds on fragile bones.

I slept well that night knowing the bad man fled,
the chain on his apartment door my only keepsake,
a chain, up high, gold-plated, beyond my reach.
His face now an oval without eyes, ears or mouth.
A king reduced to sounds: three cracks, a tumble
and a curse. Bump, bump, bump down a flight of stairs.
His landing – a bad joke. No one's laughing.
Silence falls on an empty kitchen free of Jacks.

And I lay in bed thinking "Bravo, Mama. Bravo.
You Rolling-Pin Warrior."

SHINY & SCARRED

I don't remember what I said.
I don't remember saying anything,
just remember listening to tears
shedding blood in unfriendly light.

I don't remember saying anything,
just remember a kitchen
no bigger than a closet,
Mom, no more than two steps away,
me sitting at the green Formica table,
all diamonds and chrome.

Yes, the table I remember well.

In time with the voice above me,
the chrome drove round and round,
chrome like the cars
my mother's husbands drove,
like my husbands' drive.

Tough chrome, the kind that won't break,
shiny and scarred.

To this day I don't know
if I gave her any comfort,
a kind word, a hug or a smile;
so lost was I - in a transformation,
a necessary journey,
from sacrifice to survival
from love to pity.

GHOSTING

The blood that I share, the words that cut,
I feel – in a series of images with no sound,
no title cards, just fuzzy black-and-white shots I relive.

The images, carved with a piece of glass behind my right eye,
sting. Decades have eroded the script while the scars remain.
I'm reliving the moment of transfer from love to pity.

She sits reading the letter, cheeks smeared in dried
mascara tears. I'm silent, a prisoner of pity - watching.

I'm the imperfect copy, sitting off to one side, a skinny
silhouette, knots in willful hair, elastic gone from knee hi,
mule-top clogs scuffed. My armor is watchfulness.

I see a brow imperious, deadly lids,
eyes haughty with drink,
she, so thin wrists cut
through sleeves drawing blood.

Her eyes in fumes of cheap beer,
for a second,
reflect a momentary honesty,
a confusion painful to watch.

Her fury attacks the room hoping to hurt.
They land on me. I look away.

And now my eyes see in the bathroom mirror:
a brow imperious, deadly lids, eyes haughty with drink,
me, so thin my wrists cut through sleeves drawing blood;
my eyes through fumes of cheap beer,
reflect our past and present,
a ghosting of scars.

My only way out?
I think of the wisest person I know,
the one who taught me
how to love my mother.

SHORT STORIES

MAKING AN IMPRESSION

Andalyn didn't remember getting out of the car, but there she stood in a field of mown hay, clutching her right leg under her armpit; and there it was, her yellow Toyota embracing a gray van like lovers spooning. Old habits die hard, she thought. Here she was at the scene of an accident, and she'd had enough presence of mind to get out of her vehicle with all her possessions: her purse, her car registration, even her severed leg.

She was rather proud of herself for remembering all her parts. Most of the time, she forgot something important, like her checkbook or her grocery list or enough cash for refreshments at the movie theater. She usually ended up borrowing a few bucks from a friend. She hated that about herself, being beholden to people. That usually meant she'd have to loan money to others in order to continue the karmic gift of giving.

The thought of money, on any other day, might have upset Andalyn's stomach, but curiously her stomach felt just fine today; even though she could sense that there was something wrong with the air in this part of the country. Or maybe her nose was plugged up?

She tried an old trick, holding her nostrils closed and blowing, but gave up after sniffing the air a couple of times. The texture of the air remained muted. Usually a combination of rich earth, fresh manure and hay would ripen inside her head, aggravating her allergies so that her eyes and nose would drip as bad as a hole in a roof during a rainstorm. But that wasn't the case today, and intriguing as it might be on any other day, the fact that she was upright and thinking clearly seemed more important, altogether right – unlike other moments in her life – when everything seemed wrong and out of place.

In fact, her body felt lighter than it ever had since before she grew boobs. Not only did she appreciate this new makeover, she enjoyed the intensity of sensations presented through her eyes and ears. Sights and sounds were magnified today, more so than at any other time in her life. Along the surface of the fields, colors vibrated in shades of yellows and creams, and beneath these colors, other colors rode on their backs, earthy colors from molasses to dark chocolate, while the music in them rose up to mimic their movement.

She'd been standing in the field for quite a while now, avoiding the sight in the road. She wasn't proud of her squeamishness. A cut on her finger would send her reeling to the nearest piece of furniture, dizzy and nauseated. Andalyn forced her eyes up off the ground and took a good look at the vehicles. Her Toyota looked almost obscene clinging that way to the van's gray skin. She was embarrassed for her car. The shape of them together reminded Andalyn of her favorite daydreams. My God Almighty, Andalyn was glad she hadn't been found lying in somebody's arms, all naked and juicy like that. It was enough to make her hot all over just thinking of such a scene before strangers.

Andalyn peeked at the man in the driver's seat of the van, wondering what he thought of such obscenity. She supposed he wasn't embarrassed about such things. Men usually went out of their way to invite such circumstances. Unfortunately, the man wasn't in any condition to be embarrassed about their cars' behavior. It looked to Andalyn as if the man's forehead had become part of his steering wheel, the flesh embedded in the soft leather wrappings.

No, that wasn't a man, that was a boy, a boy maybe four feet tall, straining his toes to touch the gas pedal. What a shame, he was so young. The thought of his youth disturbed Andalyn, then made her angry. What fool gave a kid keys to a car? Did he steal them? What the hell were parents doing these days allowing their children to roam about the country without supervision?

Andalyn thought it might be best to find some help. The kid might still be alive. Since she wasn't the helping kind – the kind that rushed to a bloody scene and ministered to the injured – she thought perhaps she should find someone who would be willing to lift that bloody head from the steering wheel, check the thin wrist for a pulse, and blow life-giving oxygen into collapsed lungs. Or whatever the hell those people did to stave off death for a little bit longer.

When she gazed up and down the deserted country road, she hoped to see some sign of life. There was nothing moving, either on the road or in the field behind her, not even a cow or two. The road ended at a distant hump of lava rock, its umber-ribboned lips refusing to speak to her. To her left she saw a clutch of houses on a hilltop. They looked like nice homes with nice people inside, probably families with big kids and ranch parents. Those kinds of people, she'd been told, were hard working and used to helping the hopeless.

Since she felt bored just standing there doing nothing, she hitched up her leg, tucking it tighter to her body, and on her good left leg made her way toward the nearest house. She noticed with a silent oath, that the cream pump on her left foot had a brown stain on the toe. That wasn't good. She paused and set her belongings on the side of the road, then spit on her finger. But the spit refused to stick. She stuck her finger in her mouth. She might as well have stuck her finger in the air. She felt ashamed of herself. This was no time to worry about her appearance, this was an emergency, cleaning herself up could wait.

Andalyn collected her belongings and continued her journey, while hot winds mixed with dirt and dead hay droppings blew twister tails into the air. The sun, which should have made her feel some comfort, or at least hot and sweaty, instead made her feel cold, cold right down to the toes on her remaining foot. She blamed the oddness of the weather on the bad air, and how the rightness was beginning to fade, the further she moved away from her car. But she had to do something. There was no one else available. It was up to her. How strange to think that she had something important to do.

Damnation, she thought, then said the words aloud, even though today was Sunday morning, "Damn and Double Damn." Now it was too late to catch Bernice and give her back the five bucks Andalyn owed her. Oh, hell, she supposed the money didn't matter. Andalyn imagined Bernice, at this very moment, pushing her way through people to finger quilts and rub her hands along the smooth silk of mahogany sideboards.

At that moment, Andalyn envied Bernice fiercely. There was nothing better than the charm of handmade quilts, their colors and textures, and antique furniture, furniture that fills your nostrils with a trace of age and oily lemon scent from a good furniture polish. And then of course there is the touching. Oh, my, to run your hands along smooth wood, to trace the curve of a porcelain doll's head, that was the ultimate in tactile pleasure for Andalyn, or at least as close as Andalyn ever got to those other pleasures people talk about – the ones that have to do with sex.

Anyway, Bernice didn't need Andalyn's five bucks, her husband had left her a handsome pension. Although, the thought of Bernice sneaking behind Andalyn's back and buying that tub with the clawed feet, just about made Andalyn want to throttle something. And the woman would buy the tub, too, just to spite her.

Drawing closer to the houses on the hillside, Andalyn changed her mind about the ranch people, because real ranch people didn't have white plastic fencing running around the perimeter of their houses. It was just too cute, this white plastic shit. No self-respecting rancher would dare to have a pretty fence with a pretty yard full of green, water-greedy grass and annuals that cost money – every damned year – to plant. After adjusting her leg which was getting a bit heavy, she found she'd adjusted her idea of these people and wondered if maybe she should go back to the accident.

After all, these people might not have the kind of stamina necessary to witness blood and gore. They might upchuck and be a damn nuisance. No, instead, these people might insist on calling their neighbors for advice, or invite her in for a cup of coffee, while the boy down there bled to death.

Before she'd convinced herself to turn back, someone sprinted out of the house, not even bothering to shut the door securely behind, and jogged down the graveled drive. The woman, as shapeless as a broom handle, wore one of those running costumes, black spandex running pants with florescent orange and yellow strips down the seams. Her tennis shoes looked too white to be real running shoes. Her blonde hair, brushed sternly in a ponytail, whipped behind her like the mane of a haughty thoroughbred horse.

Andalyn hurried toward her. "Hey, Lady. We need help. Hey," she shouted against the wind. The jogger ran past Andalyn and down the drive to the dirt road. Andalyn realized that the woman couldn't hear her, because she was wearing one of those fancy Walkmans.

She turned to watch the jogger trot down the graveled drive, her tight butt hardly jiggling at all. Then the woman twisted in a graceful arc to the right; and she and her cute butt headed in the wrong direction, directly up the hill, away from the accident. Andalyn wasn't surprised. She'd never had much luck getting people to pay attention to her.

The brass knocker on the door hardly made a stir in the sudden squall inside the house. Somebody was having a tizzy fit in there, bawling and boohooing until Andalyn's ears rang. Andalyn stuck her head through the opening in the door and looked around. The Florentine tiles on the floor reminded Andalyn of her favorite ice-cream toppings, silver sprinkles with finely ground chocolate.

The expensive silk wallpaper had the same shade of silver, yet the swirly pattern made Andalyn dizzy, and the walnut sideboard was just too much, too bulky for that delicate tile design. Yet the décor screamed money, and although Andalyn would have chosen a lighter piece of furniture for that hall, there was nothing better than walnut to impress people.

No one came rushing to the door, so Andalyn decided to go find out what all the ruckus was about. She followed the noise and found them in the den, a boy about five beating his head on the carpeted floor, and a tall, thin man in his underwear pacing back and forth, occasionally peeking at his son with the anxious eyes of a mother cow.

Andalyn set her leg and her purse on the marble countertop and stood beside the man. She poked his arm, "Hey, Mister. I need your help. Would you look at me, please?"

The man shivered, brushing his hand along the spot where she'd touched him. How rude, Andalyn thought. When she tried to grab his arm, she felt nothing but air as he moved away from her, his face pale and drawn. She watched him kneel beside his son. The boy was so mad, his cheeks were purple, and while thrashing about with his fists and banging his head violently on the floor, the boy managed to collect fibers from the carpet, and these fibers clung to the sweat on his forehead like hairy droplets.

What a creature, Andalyn thought, a purple, sweaty, carpet pimpled midget. Such horrific displays of passion bothered Andalyn no end. She itched to yank the boy up on his feet and spank him soundly.

"Now, Torvan. You know what Mommy says about eating ice-cream for breakfast. Let's be a good boy and finish our toast and coffee."

The boy lifted his sweaty face to glare malevolently at his father, "You can't make me."

Andalyn moved toward the man. "Listen to me, damn it. I'm talking to you."

"But son, you said you wanted to be just like Daddy."

"Well, at least call 911."

"Coffee sucks."

"How about Pop tarts? Strawberry's your favorite."

Andalyn strode over to the boy, yanked him to his feet and smacked him soundly on the bottom, three times, as hard as she could. The boy stopped bawling and the purple drained from his face.

"Now see that wasn't so bad," the boy's father said, rising to his feet and moving toward the kitchen.

For the first time since the accident, someone looked Andalyn in the eye. The boy's eyes were as moony as his father's. Andalyn didn't bother to chase after him as the boy's skinny ass tore out of the room. She passed the boy and his father in the kitchen, the boy with his little arms wrapped around his father's leg, his face pressed into the man's Fruit of the Loom butt. That's all Andalyn ever saw –

people's butts, rear ends, asses, buttocks, derrieres, behinds. So many that she was sick of the sight of fannies and wanted to wipe them off the face of the earth.

While the boy and his father bonded, Andalyn searched for the phone. It took awhile to find the damn thing. The receiver, which should have been tucked inside the black cradle of the phone jack, was missing. She found the receiver in the bathroom on the second floor. It was waiting on the vanity beside the sink, black and shiny against the white marble. Andalyn picked the phone up, admiring the receiver's large numbers coated in black on a translucent background. She wondered how much such a piece of equipment cost. Probably a lot more than she could afford, she decided.

When she moved to sit down on the toilet seat, she noticed that the translucent numbers on the keypad lit up, she could see them glow in the dusky light between the window and the partition that separated the toilet from the shower, and she thought to herself – how convenient!

Just before Andalyn propped her butt on the toilet seat, she sensed a cavity, a void where there should have been something solid. Andalyn slammed the toilet seat down and thought how typical that the toilet seat would be up. Just like a man to forget to put it down after he did his business. After getting comfortable, Andalyn pressed the numbers 911 several times, before she got through, and waited impatiently for someone to answer.

"Hello. This is Andalyn Niselmeyer. There's been an accident and we need help. A boy, this boy, he's hurt, and you need to send an ambulance right away. Hello? Are you listening to me?"

The 911 operator's nasal, noncommittal voice reminded Andalyn of her fifth-grade teacher the one who called her Joannie from the start of school until a week before Christmas break. Having been called Joannie for nearly three months, Andalyn finally had had enough. When she blew up, thereafter disgracing herself in the opinion of school authorities, she recalled the momentous moment in excruciating and vivid detail. From her seat in the back row, she'd screamed, "My name is Andalyn Niselmeyer. WOMAN. Is that so hard to remember?"

For the rest of fifth grade, Andalyn was under the watchful eye of school authorities as a potential troublemaker. The consequences were mixed though. The teacher sent her to the school counselor for therapy, but at least the teacher never forgot her name. And as a result of her explosion, the event was serendipitous. Her rebellion against authority proved fruitful, outside the classroom, generating a following made up of several shy students who attached themselves to her during recess, and used her as their spokesperson.

That is until the day, Martha Mingle, a freshman at Marshall Junior High broke Andalyn's nose, after Andalyn told her that she looked like an elephant riding a tricycle. Andalyn decided then and there to keep her big mouth shut. As a consequence, she lost her fan club and returned to her old status – one of the invisibles. Only after three decades did she find her voice again, mainly because she developed an ulcer and the shrink suggested she let off some steam.

The 911 operator repeated, "Is anyone there? Do you need help?" and Andalyn began to get really annoyed.

"Of course, I'm here. Where else would I be?" Andalyn shouted into the mouthpiece. "If you'd just shut-up for a minute, I'd be able to explain what happened. You see I was driving –"

"Calling 911 for laughs is a crime, you know." If the operator had taken the time to listen, there would have been no problem understanding Andalyn – after all she was speaking clearly with her lips practically sucking the mouthpiece, her voice crisp, and most importantly in English, not some foreign garble like those Spanish people spoke. If the mouthpiece had been a neck, it would have been the proud owner of a gigantic hickey.

"I'm aware of the penalties, Lady. Now, pay attention. There is a boy badly hurt and you need to get help here, right away. The accident happened on HUBBARD ROAD just off of Cloverdale. That's west of Cloverdale, not –"

"Whoever this is, don't be afraid," the woman said, interrupting her again. Although the woman continued to ignore Andalyn, her voice had altered. She almost sounded worried when she said, "I'm sending someone out right away. Can you hear me? Is he threatening you? If so, remain calm. Stay on the line."

Andalyn jabbed at the off button and heard the faint click disconnecting her from the woman. The phone was silent once again. Andalyn considered what more she could do, a sense of futility floating inside her heart. She wiped her germs off the keypad with toilet paper and rose to a standing position.

It was then, finally, that Andalyn realized something odd. There it was – the strange sensation, right there in the pit of her stomach. Yes. Between moments there is that humming in the ears, a floating secret eager to rise up and speak a truth. Andalyn hushed her beating heart to search out that moment, recognizing the hum in her inner ear, a hum that became a voice, and the voice spoke to her between the ticking and cracking in the back of her neck. So, this is what it's like, she thought.

Andalyn collected her purse and her leg from downstairs and left the house, returning to the scene of the accident. If she had to, she supposed she could use her blouse as a bandage and her leather belt as a tourniquet. Perhaps she was too late. She found the boy sitting on the ground in the middle of the hayfield. She moved toward him. He looked up at her.

"Hey, do you hear a humming?" she asked him.

"I have a special driver's permit," he told her.

"Really. That's nice."

"Those are my folks over there. You see them."

Andalyn turned. A tractor was parked on the side of the road. A man in overalls and a sweaty cowboy hat pulled the boy's body out of the van, while his wife spread an old wool blanket on the ground. The man gently rested the boy's body on the blanket, and together they knelt beside him, hugging each other.

"They look tough," Andalyn said. The boy nodded lifting a piece of straw to his lips and biting down hard.

"So, what should we do?" Andalyn asked him, sitting down beside him to rest her leg and her purse in her lap.

"I'm sorry I hit you. I didn't mean to. I was trying to avoid a jogger."

"Makes sense."

"Where were you?"

Andalyn looked into his eyes. It was nice to make an impression for the second time in her life. "I was trying to get help. My first time."

"That should count for something," he said, rising to walk over to his parents. Andalyn watched him press his face to their backs. Then he did a strange thing. He moved inside them and didn't come out.

Andalyn looked around. This place felt so deep and wide. Without buildings to block her view, she could see for miles. Open spaces used to make her nervous. Yet, here she was, sitting in a field – all alone – and she didn't feel a bit scared.

Her car was a sorry sight. Did she love her car that much? Well, no. Not that much. Unlike the boy, Andalyn had to rule out close kin: her parents were dead, she'd never married, and she didn't have any kids. How about Bernice? No. That wouldn't work. Bernice loves fiercely and isn't very discriminating in her taste. Even her rude neighbors, and the rottweiler living at the end of her block receive samplings of her habitual good will. To love that way would drive Andalyn crazy.

In the back of Andalyn's mind, an old nervousness crawled across her scalp. She'd have to make a decision soon, and what if she made the wrong one? Then Andalyn remembered how the sun felt on her head, warming the top and spreading down her neck to her back. Something like that was happening right now. It felt damn good.

In fact, Andalyn felt so good, she wanted to share her pride and euphoria. Andalyn noticed the jogger standing on the other side of the road. The woman had been there for some time, rubbing her arms as if she were cold and craning her neck to see beyond the shoulders of the farm couple. For the first time, Andalyn acknowledged the fact that perhaps she wasn't the only one who might be feeling a bit lonely.

Andalyn decided to get up off her butt and go comfort her. Without thinking things through Andalyn moved toward the woman, hugged her tight, and as a reward felt the tightness loosen inside herself. The woman started to cry. Andalyn separated herself from the jogger, exhausted by such intense energy and overwhelming guilt. The woman moved toward the farm couple, and knelt beside them, her wail mixing with the wail of sirens.

Andalyn was no longer blood and bone – she realized that at last. She'd even forgot to carry her leg with her this time. It must have been back there in the upstairs bathroom, when she first acknowledged a portion of the truth. Now Andalyn wanted to be a part of something, something that would last forever.

The Owyhee Mountains, just beyond the Snake River, were only ten miles away. And beyond the Owyhees, there were miles and miles of open spaces. Yet right here, right now, the earth moved beneath her, and hummed a familiar tune. She liked the feel of this land, and the sound the sun made along her spine. She decided to head toward the lava-rock mound in the distance. That hump along the top of the mound reminded Andalyn of her father's shoulder. She remembered that he used to carry her through the fairgrounds on his wide shoulders, and she felt so proud that she could see above the crowd, see all the rides, the stalls, the people.

Perhaps she'd hug a rock and disappear inside for a time.

STREET RATS

The others were waiting where they were most comfortable – in the dark. Jodi stood beneath the smoking streetlight dressed in purple silk pants and a green blouse. The streetlight was the only illumination for several miles. The city could afford just one gas powered streetlight for each neighborhood; yet, the wealthy managed to find enough fuel to keep all eighteen floors of this building, including the lighted blue fins, lit all day and night.

In this neighborhood those still free to roam preferred the safety of the dark. Jodi's curly red hair, like the flames inside the streetlight's globe, were on fire. The strands of her hair and the flickering flames moved in syncopation. The children especially loved to touch her hair. They were convinced the color coincided with a dim memory of warmth.

Everyone who had been in hiding squirmed to the very edge of the alley exposing themselves to the light's glare, just for a better view of Jodi. The caretaker in charge of the children rose to her feet and attempted to separate herself from them. She was forced to peel desperate fingers from her shoulders then her legs. She heard a nearly forgotten sound. As the contraption moved closer, the throbbing intensified. It was rare to see such vintage items in her neighborhood.

The caretaker forced herself to walk, not run, toward the sound. She strolled past Jodi with a glance and a nod. A silver car shaped like a bullet pulled up beside the red head. Jodi leaned forward to talk to the driver. The caretaker passed the vehicle and outside the streetlight's glow abruptly dropped to the ground. She scrambled on all fours behind the vehicle straining to hear Jodi as she massaged the price.

"A loaf of bread. Real baked bread. From the oven."

"What? You mistake me for a baker? I'm no baker. I got coin."

"Monies no good here."

"How about a nice warm jacket? Real fleece."

Loose chunks of crumbling tar dug into the caretaker's knees. She touched the motor carriage feeling the cold metal beneath her fingertips. From the exhaust pipe a noxious smell made her head spin.

Only the very rich were permitted to drive these ancient carriages on city streets.

Jodi laughed at something the driver said.

The caretaker knew only what she needed to know about gas powered cars – that they needed fuel to run and they were vulnerable in several places. The caretaker hadn't seen a car like this for years. It wasn't the parts she coveted. There were graveyards full of these metal skeletons all over the city. It wasn't its fuel she needed either. The air they breathed had more dirty particles than this old fart. Come morning the sun's light would attempt to penetrate the foul eye-stinging air only to recede in defeat. There was a time when daylight meant something, but daylight meant nothing anymore to those who lived on the streets.

She knelt near the rear driver's side tire and plunged the point of her blade into the rubber. She stabbed at the tire several times to be sure. Once satisfied with her work, the caretaker slipped her blade inside her coat pocket and returned to the sidewalk. She feigned confusion weaving her way toward the vehicle with her hands out.

"Can you help me, Ma'am?" she asked. "I'm lost."

Jodi glanced over her shoulder and murmured to the driver, "Just a moment, Lordy. Let me get rid of this pissant oozing poison." Straightening to her full height her green eyes sneered down at the old woman.

The caretaker stretched her neck and swallowed several times slipping from a high-pitched whine to a frightened mumble, "I've been looking up and down this street for hours. I need the caretaker. You know him?"

Jodi spit out her gum, "Do I look like a map?"

The caretaker wandered toward the open window of the silver car and ducked her head inside, "Maybe you got more manners than this whore, noble Lordy. You know where I can find the sanctuary, the one that ain't run by the brainfuckers?"

The driver leaned forward his bulldog of a face reflected in the yellow glare of the streetlight. The caretaker looked into his eyes. He was furious at having been interrupted. She struggled to control her loathing. His smug arrogance sent tiny currents of rage roiling through her body. The rage woke them up.

As if she'd lit a fire under them, the sparklers began to seek a way out. Their white heat seared first the back of her head, then the temples. The struggle to control them wore down her depleted reserves. Her hungry old body began to tremble. He didn't seem to notice.

She had to hold on. Just another minute. It meant so much to the others. Just let go. If she touched him, the pain would seek a new body. She had no reason to touch him. Something about her struggle to control her inner revulsion pleased him. The caretaker kept smiling, even though his pleasure in her pain seemed to arouse him. The thought that he might be into little old ladies repulsed her.

"The sanctuary you say. Hum. The name sounds familiar. You want to step inside, and we can discuss this further," he said leaning over to open the door. His suntanned skin hid the parasite within. The caretaker had only a second to decide what to do. She would regret her decision, regret not following her instincts warning her to go back to the children.

She grabbed his thick-fingered hairy hand and connected her flesh with his flesh. Images flicked past her mind's eye, images of sunshine atop a skyscraper and a pool filled with clean water. His lived experience exploded inside her. In retaliation she sent her memories through his nerve endings and into his bloodstream.

So, he wanted to see how long he could survive the Reeky Bottom without suffocating or boiling alive, huh? Oh, yeah. Let's see what a big man you are, netdevil. Here we go my pasty-faced friend. Here's what it's like to starve as your blood boils. He screamed and jerked his arm away tucking it safely within the shelter of the car. The motion rocked her forward nearly sending her headfirst through the open window and onto his lap. Behind her she heard the children flapping their arms wildly, flesh meeting brick.

A few seconds after the caretaker detached herself from the rich troll, she recognized the shapes swarming about them, people in uniforms, booted feet, guns pointed at her, and her final vision – Jodi between two suits their faces obscured by rebreathers. She saw Jodi struggling to free herself from their painful embrace.

The coolness of the room and the richness of the oxygen forced the caretaker's body to adapt in painful humiliating ways. She heard the female doctor say to the attendant, "What's her condition?" The blinding light, unfamiliar sounds and absence of smells brought back old memories, old terrors. She had been the target all along. They should have moved to a new location. Why did she listen to Jodi? Why did she let those damn kids influence her? She'd survived all these years because she kept to herself, avoiding the light, avoiding the attention of the suits.

"All the monitors are telling me her heart stopped and her brain is dead," said the attending nurse. The caretaker didn't know his name. No one used their names. No one expressed anger or revulsion. Someone had warned them, some traitor, maybe? Or had they tortured one of the street rats? The nurse was as much a part of the furniture as the bed the caretaker lay on. His attempt at humor failed to generate a response from the doctor.

The caretaker could feel the doctor's vexation. It was clouding her judgement, but would it be enough to generate a connection between them? The caretaker had been preparing everyone for this day. She'd trained the children. They had shot right past her attaining unheard of levels, some, capable of using the enemy's emotions to inoculate themselves against capture. Others, if they failed could submerge themselves in past lives free from malware. Jodi could easily manage several months of dormancy. She, on the other hand, was getting too old. Her mind would eventually betray her.

When she was young hospitals were run by doctors and nurses. Just as national parks had once been run by park rangers. The great purge changed everything. There was no one to take care of the people or the woodlands, so the few who survived decided to repurpose parks and hospitals. Today parks are where the cars go to die. Now, the buildings where babies had been born, the sick were healed and the old went to die belonged to programmers and prison guards.

The primary function of hospitals was to program the street rats into obedient soldiers and slaves. Soldiers no longer fought in foreign wars. Instead, soldiers fought for the rich and risked their lives hunting big game. Since metal corroded if immersed in oceans, rivers and lakes, street rats were trained to dive down into the dark depths to find food. After all, street rats were perfect Reeky Bottom dwellers. They could breathe the air below and drink the tainted water without getting sick and dying.

The caretaker knew she was too old and sick to be a candidate for a slave or a soldier. They needed her to lure the street rats to the hospital. Her present programming nurse was assigned to keep an eye on her and notify the programmers when she showed signs of life. She could feel the needle in her arm and the pads at her temples. The restraints bound her wrists and ankles to the bed posts. It was a familiar sensation. She'd been here before, years ago.

"She can't stay dead forever," the doctor corrected him.

The caretaker felt the momentum slip and her death evaporating. She had once shut herself down for a year. It had been during the second wave when the bombs hit Alaska and sent a mushroom cloud spewing radioactive dust everywhere. The fallout covered the Northwest. It had been a fluke. Weather patterns and winds. She'd found a burrow which once had been the home of badgers. A year. She'd shut herself down for a year. Could she do it again?

But now, there was something in the air, something different, the smells were familiar, reminding her of her childhood, old memories, good memories, a better time when there was plenty of food and sunshine and clean air. Why were the Four Families allowing their employees to bake cookies and smoke cigarettes? It took several hours to fight off the memory of a time when being alive had been a good thing. The smells were too tempting, they slipped behind her defensive wall.

The female doctor and the male nurse stood above her and watched as she allowed her eyes to accept the images. She saw them from several angles, from her prone position on the bed and from the ceiling. Those dual views would subside once she decided to be in the room and aware of them. The doctor and the nurse expressed mutual amazement and hope. Their hope gave her the courage to lick her lips and speak.

Her vocal cords had relaxed into their accustomed shape, "The baked cookies are a nice touch."

The nurse nodded, his mouth curving as if ready to smile, "Thought you would like it."

"What's your name?" she asked him.

"Steve."

"You human?"

"Of course. I wouldn't be here otherwise."

The caretaker allowed herself to sleep. In her dream the restraints were removed and the skin on her forehead and temples cleaned with soap and oil. To be human is to be a natural predator, a sometime killer, yet, always determined to stay alive. They assumed she was a helpless old fart who would give in. They were mistaken. She would fight back in the only way she knew how. She sent the poison coursing through her veins and waited. She feigned a normal sleep pattern.

The nurse removed the pins which were keeping her eyelids open. Even with his safety gloves on, the poison slipped beyond the barrier, through his skin and into his bloodstream. The infection would spread like the common cold, everyone exposed to the street-rat virus and no one aware until it was too late. The programmers would lose all their data. The people would be free. She began to dream. She hadn't dreamt since she was a little girl. She saw herself swinging through the air. The toes of her tennis shoes reached for the sun.

CHINESE JUMP ROPE

Whenever a gust of wind blew down the street, the little hairs on my neck felt as if invisible fingers were tickling them. My ponytail, in the iron grip of a green rubber band was so tight, my eyes felt Chinese. Chinese eyes, Chinese Jump Rope, I thought. My friends, Gwen and Connie held each end of the thick red and blue rubber bands. In the shadow cast by the Maple, my friends looked like statues kneeling on the pavement, one cool shade, the other sunlight on chrome. Each held one end of the Chinese Jump Rope keeping the corners tight and in the shape of a rectangle.

"Well?' Gwen asked. "Have you got any ideas?"

"No," I told her, pausing to catch my breath. "But I've still got time." I leaned forward, resting my hands on my knees and watched the sweat drip from my forehead to the ground. "You know you guys don't have to come in if you don't want to."

"We know," Gwen said.

I waited, giving them a chance to take off. Nobody moved.

"Thanks," I said at no one in particular.

"Any time," Connie shot back convinced I'd been talking to her.

It was the summer of '68. Three months had passed since the assassination of Martin Luther King. Over in Vietnam, thousands of soldiers were dying. In the Melville and Peterson households, the women in my family were dying too. I could sense them corroding inside, while little bits of fear and tension flaked off their souls everyday, leaving bare nerves exposed. They suffered, and I, in angry self-defense built a fortress to keep them from taking me down with them. Books were my best weapon. I could lose myself in the past and forget the present. The past was known, the present full of shadows.

When we first arrived at Aunt Corrinne's house after breakfast, the present intruded into our lives, nearly biting a chunk out of the peacefulness around Corinne's green Formica-top kitchen table. Grandma had gotten to Corrinne's house first and whatever she'd told her daughter must have been super important because they both had twin frowns on their faces when we entered the room.

Grandma Ona took charge that morning since Aunt Corrinne ignored us and just stared out the window smoking her cigarette. With her daughters and grandkids milling about the kitchen, Grandma Ona told me and my friends to fetch the matching Formica leaf from the attic. Even with the leaf the table couldn't hold us all.

The heat from the kitchen stove drove the kids into the living room, some to spread themselves out on the floor in front of the brand-new big screen color tv. They looked like a jumble of discarded toys. The nearsighted had scooted so close to the television their noses were practically touching the screen. Soon my Aunt Corrinne appeared carrying a tray of snacks. Close behind her came my mother balancing a small stack of party cups in one hand and a lit cigarette between her slim fingers. Her fingernails were as bright and shiny as fresh blood.

Everybody ended up in the living room and when my cousins realized the adults were getting ready for a good gossip, they escaped outside. The uneasiness in the air bothered me so much I decided to stay and learn why my grandmother looked so scared.

The suspense was killing me as they lit cigarettes and poured themselves drinks. The uneasiness had something to do with the letter in Grandma Ona's hand. Because I wanted desperately to wipe away the worry in my grandma's eyes, I blurted out the first thing that came into my head. "This Fall we'll be learning how to dance in gym class, and I don't know how. What am I going to do? I'll be the biggest geek in the room, I know it."

The diversion worked. It worked so well, my cry for help escalated into a major campaign. At least I hadn't been stupid enough to ask where babies came from. Grandma Ona would have been suspicious right away and Mom would have been eager to fill me in on all the grizzly details. Even after health class, I preferred Ona's version. Ona hadn't stuttered or looked uncomfortable like Mrs. Gould.

"Is sex bad?"

"No," Ona said.

"Then how come the Bible says it's bad?"

"The Bible doesn't say it's bad," Ona snapped.

"Do you like sex, Grandma?"

"Yes. It takes time, but when you love someone," Ona began and stopped, not because she was embarrassed but because she was thinking about something else.

"Like you loved Grandpa," I spoke into the silence hoping she'd return to me.

"Like I loved Grandpa," Ona said. "It's wonderful. Give yourself time. You need to grow up some. You'll understand what I mean when you're older."

When I asked Grandma's renter Andrew Stockton who lived in the upstairs apartment right above my ground floor bedroom the same question, he didn't blush or stammer either. "You bet I do, Curly. It's far out; better than that, it's out of sight."

It was my first experience with a body rush of jealousy so intense my knees trembled. "Is it Kathy? Do you love Kathy?"

"I thought you liked Kathy?" Andrew asked.

I had to admit I did like Kathy, but that was before I knew the truth. Now I wasn't so sure. To please him, I agreed to like Kathy. Even if I had had an older brother or a father at home, which I didn't, I still would have asked Andrew if sex was bad. I valued his opinion and his wisdom about the ways of the world. He knew important facts, like the fact that if I wanted to fly jets, I would need to take extra math classes, blood was blue, and a quick kick to the knee was more dignified than pulling someone's hair.

Yet his last piece of advice wasn't as easy to understand or accept. It had come out of nowhere, for no good reason, and made me uncomfortable. "Try to remember Curly that crying isn't bad. Don't buy into their crap that crying is for babies. Crying just proves you're human."

His odd remark troubled me, like a cryptic code I couldn't decipher. He couldn't have been talking about me. That was silly, because I cry sometimes. Just the other day, I cried when I fell and scraped my knees on the sidewalk. The time I bit my tongue, I cried a lot, especially the day I slammed my finger in the car door. If he meant the other kind of crying, the self-pitying kind, I did that in my room, late at night with a pillow over my head. I wasn't proud of it and hoped someday when I was older and more mature, I wouldn't need to cry anymore.

Maybe his remark had nothing to do with me. Maybe it had to do with Kathy blubbering all over Andrew's navy jacket at the airport? Standing next to them had been my Uncle Pete wearing the same navy jacket as Andrew. They had been drafted at the same time. They both chose the Navy like all the men in their families before them. They had been friends forever. Andrew looked sad, sad for his girlfriend Kathy. My uncle looked terrified as if he was afraid to get on the plane and fly back to boot camp. The fear in his eyes made no sense.

Uncle Pete loved to fly. Uncle Pete once jumped off Grandma's roof to see if he could fly. At the time, I wasn't paying much attention to Uncle Pete's twitchy behavior, my eyes were full of Andrew's girlfriend slobbering all over his beautiful jacket, kissing his neck and acting like a moron. He didn't seem to mind. Andrew wasn't like other guys, but even the good ones acted geeky around their girlfriends.

While waves of heat floated up from the sidewalk and the smell of hot tar, clipped grass and exhaust fumes hung in the air, I danced with the Chinese Jump Rope and wondered if Gwen ever cried. As far as I knew I'd never seen Gwen cry, at least not in public.

Anyway, Gwen wasn't the crying kind; she was tough. I'd always wanted to be just as tough. Even though my feet were callused from walking barefoot everywhere, the heat from the pavement interrupted my concentration, burning so much I wanted to give in. Instead, I thought about the two toughest people I knew, Gwen and Andrew. Their examples reminded me that true courage meant keeping my feet on the ground.

The rubber band stretched over the arch of my right foot, rubbing on my dirty ankle raising a welt. I ignored the stinging pain. With each step my thick ponytail nipped and slapped my sunburned skin. Trickling sweat poured down my body like Niagara Falls, soaking the waist band of my green peddle-pushers. I fought the urge to scratch the spot, the brand-new spot where my skin and the training bra refused to meet. That area was an exit ramp for all the sweat pouring down my neck. If I'd been alone, I might have taken a quick swipe, but never, absolutely never, in public.

When a guy driving a blue Mustang turned onto my street, revving his engines as he passed, smoking and singing the lyrics to a Beatle's song, I froze embarrassed at nearly being caught tugging, scratching and poking in public. I heard the guy sing "take a sad song and make it better" and started to giggle.

Gwen and Connie joined in. Even though we agreed he'd been cute we also agreed his voice sucked. Thanks to my Mom I'd prevented a major disaster. If the Mustang Guy and my friends had seen me doing something so uncool as the TSPs, my faux pas would have beaten his bad voice and I would have wanted to melt into the cement, a puddle of sweat, right there on the sidewalk like the witch in Wizard of Oz.

The loud bang of the screen door, like the recess bell at school warned us the fun was at an end. It was time to face the music, literally. My mother, a thin dark woman dressed in cut-offs and t-shirt pulled a lit Marlboro out of her mouth and said, "It's time, Jean. Hurry up." I often wonder why my mother sounds angry even when she's in a good mood.

I missed my pass, tangled my feet in the rope and fell. Gwen gathered up the rope and calmly draped it around her long slender neck. In my overworked imagination, Gwen resembled a priestess preparing for battle. If Gwen's Chinese Jump Rope and Connie's St.

Christopher medal had any power at all, I wished they would start producing some results soon. I pretended a calmness I didn't feel and rose to my feet brushing the grass off my knees.

The three of us walked single file into Aunt Corinne's house, me in the lead. Connie, at the end of the line, dragged her feet, chewing on the stub of a fingernail with a worried face. What was she worried about? She wasn't the sacrificial lamb.

The coffee table, ottoman and magazine rack had been shoved into the next room. Two women stood on the orange rug in their bare feet, waiting for me to appear with duel expressions of serene contemplation. They were sisters. The tallest, my mother Amanda, appeared tough on the outside, but an unkind word from a stranger could shatter her entire day. At least when the unkind word or anger was directed at her. When the anger wasn't directed at her, my mother could be brave, sometimes to the point of suicidal.

That was one kind of toughness. The other kind stood beside Amanda, pale and thin in baggy peddle-pushers and a short-sleeved silk blouse. Corinne appeared fragile, but nothing short of a typhoon could move her an inch from her rock of self-confidence. Nobody dared manipulate her or they got an earful, sometimes an elbow too.

The sight of them standing side by side reminded me of pictures straight out of National Geographic. The sisters were members of an ancient tribe, eager to pass down their traditions to the next generation. In my case, the tradition was the complex art of a dance called the jitterbug. I swallowed a painful giggle.

When my mother beamed in my direction, I no longer felt like laughing. No, this wasn't funny. It was going to be unbearable, worse than a visit to the dentist. I had a sudden urge to run upstairs and lock myself in the bathroom. As usual my legs refused to budge.

When Aunt Corinne dropped the needle onto the 45 and old people's music floated through the room and out the open windows, I wondered if Mustang Man was sneering at Buddy Holly. I didn't want to chicken out especially in front of my friends. Yet my muscles betrayed me tightening in terror. I can't do it. I can't. Not in front of Gwen and Connie.

My mother grabbed my wrist and pulled me toward the center of the room, "Honey. This won't hurt a bit. Loosen up. Come on. Shake it off."

Aunt Corinne spun on tiptoe to face the room her graceful arms lifted theatrically in the air. I saw Aunt Corinne smiling and having fun and I made the biggest mistake of my life. "I want Corinne to teach me, Mom," I told her, desperate to gain time and maybe distract everybody.

My mother's smile faded, "Sure."

I no longer felt my mother's fingers on my wrist and instantly regretted hurting her. Before I could form an apology, Grandma Ona turned to Gwen, "How about it, Gwen? You want to learn the jitterbug?"

Gwen, too late to make a run for the door, turned slowly to face the room. I admired her composure. "Sure, Mrs. Melville. I'll give it a try." No matter how silly the situation, whether scaling the ledge of Webster Elementary on a dare and making it all the way to the front or spitting soda through her nose, Gwen never turned into a puddle of sweat.

Joey, my youngest cousin stopped chewing the rubber around the rail of his playpen long enough to voice his approval by clapping his hands and squealing gibberish. Grandma Ona lifted him out of the playpen and set him on her hip so that he might have a better view. Ona's blue eyes drilled holes into my brain daring me to flee. I sensed the room was on Mama's side and learning to dance the jitterbug was the cross I had to bear.

"You said you wanted to learn how to dance. Remember?" Ona reminded me.

I tried another ploy, "I don't know. Maybe I don't need to learn. Maybe I can skip dance until next year." I met Ona's challenge with a whimper. Long after the nightmare was over, I would think about that day and wish I'd been more daring.

"Did I ever tell you the story about Pete's worst weekend?" Ona asked as she bounced Joey on her hip.

"It's just a stupid dance, not a deer hunt, Grandma."

"The fears the same."

The screen door banged in chorus with the drumming of the music. One, two, three, four. Once they were on the move, they sounded like a herd of rhinos running toward water. My cousins; Matt, Michael, Michele and Martin burst into the room and skidded to a stop a few feet behind Ona. Identical dirty faces mirrored surprise at the condition of the living room and the way the adults were so gleeful. Matt's expressive face registered eager anticipation; I knew what he was thinking. At eight years old, he was at the age when moments of humiliation and depravity were highlights in his young life. The more humiliating for someone else, the better.

I itched to wipe the smirk off his face. Unlike Matt, his sister Michele looked as if she were attending a funeral, her little hands clasped in front of her, mouth frowning. She probably sensed her day was coming soon enough.

Gwen and Amanda whirled about the room, Gwen's low throaty laughter following in their wake. Aunt Corinne reached for my hand. I backed away and said, "I can't. Not with the rug-rats watching."

I gestured at my cousins as if their snickering were the best evidence needed to set me free. Corinne's smile disappeared and she asked with hands on her hips, "Does it really matter?"

"I can't do this. It'll be different anyway. You know it'll be boys and."

"You might be right. Maybe Connie wants to learn."

Matt, face screwed up in a sneer of disdain, chanted over the music, "Jean's a chicken. Jean's a chicken. Bok...Bah...Bok!"

Ona headed for the kitchen. I couldn't stand the disappointment in the room; I gave in, "Okay, I'll do it."

Once I turned down Ona's offer of ice cream, the room cleared of tiny tot terrors. Corinne didn't give me another chance to back out of the dance lesson. She clasped my hand firmly and demonstrated the steps. With stiff limbs drained of nerve, I tried to mimic her moves, and at the same time, I tried to ignore Matt's chocolate sneer and rolling eyes. I kept my balance by luck alone and jitterbugged until the chime of the doorbell ended my first lesson.

Grateful for the interruption, I ran for the front door. I was the first to fling it back and see Uncle Pete in his uniform standing on the stoop. I was also the first to see the tears and the shame when he realized his mother and his sisters were in the room. The angry screech of the needle sliding across the 45 ended the music.

There was silence, a silence so painful I could hear Pete gasping. The MP's standing between him looked like redwood trees between a sapling. My mother pushed me out of the way. I stumbled back feeling a solid wall behind me.

My mother's body effectively blocked my view of Pete and the MPs. I felt like a potted plant decorating the hallway, a potted plant with ears. "What's going on Pete? What's wrong?" my mother asked her voice rising an octave.

"Peter Melville is AWOL, Ma'am. We'd like to talk to his mother."

Aunt Corinne marched to the door and stood beside her sister her face pinched in disgust as if she'd swallowed a bug.

I felt the nightmare take hold. It darkened the room and deafened the sound. I felt as if the oxygen had been sucked out of the room. I held my arms tight to my chest. People were talking over each other and the decibel level hurt my eardrums. Still within the babble, words began to make sense.

"Murderers."
"Circling the block."
"Leave him alone."
"Tomorrow back to Camp-"
“He’s staying here with us. You can’t.”

I thought I had myself under control until I made the mistake of turning to look at the others standing on the orange oval rug listening and staring at the MPs. In that moment I saw Gwen take Joey out of Ona's arms and head for the kitchen. I saw Connie hesitate for a second, switching her weight from one foot to the other, then run after Gwen biting her thumb nail to the quick.

That left Grandma Ona, Ona all alone in the middle of the orange rug. I couldn't look away. In my left ear the voices of Mom and Aunt Corinne shouted and cursed washing over my head, no longer making sense. The MPs voices chimed in trying to be heard over the women’s furious defense of their brother. Somewhere in the middle, Pete struggled to cough up words drowning in his tears.

It was Grandpa's funeral all over again. A room packed with hysterical women weeping all over the casket, men comforting their wives and Grandma Ona in the center of the room, stiff, standing in skinless fear, her nerves all exposed, with nobody touching her for fear of infection. The fringe around the orange rug was like a perimeter, a demarcation zone preventing her from stepping outside the oval. Nobody so much as stepped inside the circle to comfort her.

I remember hating them, wishing they would go away and leave her alone. I didn't cry then, and I was damned sure I wasn’t going to cry ever again. Without quite knowing how, I found myself beside her. When I tried to touch her, she pushed me away. "Is it bad to cry, Grandma?"

She looked at me as if I’d been a stranger asking her an impertinent question. I tried again, "Is it bad to cry?"

I plunged my hands through the coldness between us and wrapped my arms around her, hanging on for dear life. I could hear her heart drumming in my ear. She was Halston, baby powder, cinnamon and soft pillows. I tried to hold the tears back, but Andrew's words were ringing in my head. I wanted to be human.

THE CLEAN UP CREW

Clifford Judge sliced off three thick hunks of deer meat. With each stroke of his blade, the garage quivered with tension. He wiped the blood off his blade onto his hip, streaking his mud caked blue jeans with bright slashes of red. He turned to face three pairs of eyes. Their eyes never left his face, reminding him of knotholes in cherry wood, expressing nothing around the rim and everything in the black.

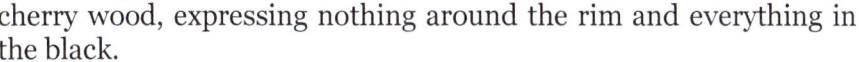

From their bodies came a humming. He dropped to his knees and placed the three pieces of meat on the floor, then walked outside. Their slick, black bodies visibly trembled in anticipation. He stopped to lean against the front fender of his truck and crossed his arms. "Dinner's Ready." A blur of black bodies lunged for the meat. Judge watched with affectionate pride as fangs tore into the bloody chunks.

Judge thought about open fields, mountain ridges and green valleys. He couldn't wait to get out of town. Here, there were too many people crowding him, nosy, talkative neighbors with nothing better to do then spy through curtains and cluck behind his back. Like his crew, Judge needed running room, wood smoke and the taste of blood in his mouth.

10

"Don't Bill. I'm eating, damned it," Millie Morris growled, looking down at her plate of pancakes and sausages. Bill ignored her warning and pulled a booger out of his nose wiping the slimy green creature off his finger and onto the edge of the ashtray near old cigarette butts. Millie hated the ashtray, almost as much as she despised Bill. The ashtray was a Father's Day gift from their son Dillon. Millie thought the ashtray looked more like a cow-pie than a horseshoe, and she often wondered if the ashtray was Dillon's idea of a joke.

Five minutes passed. Millie looked up from her plate. The seat opposite was empty. She stared at the ashtray for a long time before she rose to her feet.

Hot water rushing out of the shower head drowned out the creak of the bathroom door. On the other side of the shower curtain, her husband cleared his throat to spit. Millie's lips twitched uncontrollably. She thrust the shower curtain aside and lifted her arm above her head.

In the time it took to blink, her eyes traveled from her husband's flabby white legs, up his hairy back to his short thick neck where the pale flesh stopped, and the reddish-brown leathery skin began. His head was bent, his finger covering one nostril. He blew hard and a gob of white mucous dropped near his bare toe and slid down the drain.

With a rush of pleasure so intense her knees wobbled; she brought her arm down with all the force in her upper body. She struck him on the side of his head just above his ear. He dropped to his knees. She hit him again, harder. Her arm rose to strike one more time. Blood spurted from the open wound staining a violent rhythm onto the pink tiles. When her wrist began to throb painfully, she stopped, cradling her arm to her belly.

The gnawing anger in the pit of her stomach vanished. While the blood ran down the drain, she left the bathroom and returned to the kitchen to finish her breakfast. When she passed the stainless-steel sink, she slipped the bloody ceramic ashtray in the soapy water. Just like the man to pick a fight with her on a Monday morning.

9

Dillon woke to the sound of the phone ringing. He grabbed for the receiver smacking his hand against the sharp edge of the hardwood bedside table. “Shit. Hello. Mom? What?”

The voice on the other end was shriller than usual, “I said meet me down at the new site in an hour. Your Dad. Well, um. He's sick and I'm going to do the pouring today in his place.”

“Sure, Mom. I'll see you there.”

“Good. Be sure to eat something that'll stick to your ribs. It's colder than a witch's tit outside.”

He listened to the drone of the phone for a few seconds, then carefully dropped the receiver in its cradle. Dusty, his new friend turned over on her side and smiled seductively. “What's your Mom want, sweetie?”

“Wants me to meet her at the site.” Her look of disappointment pleased him. He leaned over to kiss her. The phone rang again. He groaned and picked up the phone on the third ring, recognizing his cousin's voice on the other end, “Hey there, Casanova. What's up?”

“There's been a change in plans, Dillon,”

Dillon sat up and tucked his pillow behind his back listening to his cousin's voice drone on and on and on about nothing important. The guy loved to talk about himself.

When Dillon hung up the phone, he swung his legs off the bed. "Sorry, Babe. Got to get up. Guess we'll take care of business tonight." He stood up and stretched then debated whether to call his mother back and pretend to be sick. "Holy shit," he gasped. It finally dawned on him what his mother had said. They were pouring the foundation today. "No. No."

He grabbed his dirty pants off the floor from yesterday and hopped into them on his way to the bathroom. "No. No. Hell, no."

"What's wrong, sweetie?" Dusty asked concerned as she heard him hitting the wall and slamming doors. When he reappeared thrusting his arms through his black leather jacket, she grew alarmed. "I got to go. Make yourself some breakfast. See you tonight. Bye," he said absently, throwing the bedroom door open and stumbling down the stairs. Swinging her legs off the bed, she pulled the bedroom curtain aside to watch him hop on his Harley and kick the starter so savagely she thought his foot was going to stab a hole in the street.

8

Six hours ago, Amanda had been standing beside her car, tapping her cute gold high-heeled shoe, little lines of impatience cutting into the contours of her brand-new nose and rosebud lips. The silky red evening gown plastered to her body revealed all the curves he loved so much. Her bosom heaved with every breath she took. In excited anticipation, he watched them rise and fall, hoping they would pop right out, and she would run into his arms consumed with passion at the sight of him.

No such luck though. When he looked into those brilliant blue eyes stabbing him with their coldness, he realized she was drunk. The cops had booted her car tire and the first words out of her mouth were, "I need a drink."

With patience and persistence, he managed to get her inside his apartment for one last drink. Propped on the edge of his couch, she crossed one silk leg over the other, and snapped a piece of gum between pearly white teeth. He offered her a glass of wine with a trembling hand. Before gulping down his best Chardonnay, she stuck her gum on the rim and took a hefty gulp. He gritted his teeth at the sight. Why couldn't she be as classy as she looked?

"So where are you off to tonight?" he asked, swirling the wine in his glass.

"That's none of your," she sighed. "Well, hell. I'm going to a party. You mind? My boss asked me to come. It's his birthday. You know what I mean?"

He lifted his eyes from his glass. Her head swiveled from one side of the room to the other, from the ceiling fan to the rug. She glanced at his black and white photos on the wall then the bear-skin rug. He flushed hotly when she curled her lip at the rug. That was where they kissed for the first time. When he realized she wanted him as much as he wanted her, he thought he'd gone to heaven.

That had been months ago. It felt like years. Perhaps the sex had been uninspiring for her, but for him, the sex had been life changing. Even the women at his company were giving him second looks.

He thought about all the money he'd spent on Amanda and the late nights waiting for her phone call. He'd been patient with her. He'd listened to her daily bitching about her coworkers and boss for months before he offered a few sensible suggestions. She turned down his suggestion to come work for him as his personal secretary. She claimed she had a lot of years invested in her job and didn't want to risk her pension. Pension? Was she serious? She wasn't old enough to have accrued much of a pension. He should have known she'd been lying to him.

She'd been using him the whole time. The realization sent the acid churning in his stomach up into his esophagus. His euphoria at seeing her on the roadside tonight on his way down the mountain fizzled away replaced with a confused mix of self-loathing and pent up rage. In two swallows she finished the wine, set the glass on the coffee table and jumped to her feet. "I got to go. See you around, Ronnie." She started toward the door wobbling like a trapeze artist on the high wire in her stupid high heeled shoes.

"No. Don't leave yet. You've got time. The party doesn't start for an hour. I'll call a cab. The cab will be here in no time," he begged jumping up from the couch and walking toward her. She paused near the door. He grabbed her shoulder and swung her around.

She shrugged his hand off impatiently, glaring at him, "I got to go, Ronnie." For the first time that night, she looked at him. Whatever she saw made her angry. "You're crazy, you know that? It was just one fucking night."

"It was more than that, Amanda. It was meant to be."

"Now you really are talking nuts." She twisted around to grab for the doorknob. He pulled her away from the door and tried to wrestle her into his arms.

"You know that's not true, Amanda. We love each other. You're just scared, that's all."

She struggled to break free, "Let me go, you nut job. I don't love you. Don't you get it? I thought we had an understanding. Shit. It was just one night."

"But there can be more," he gasped trying to hold her squirming body in his arms. "Give me a chance. I know I can make you happy. Just listen to me."

He yanked her head back. Her face expressed disgust. It hurt so much to see this side of her. She'd always been so sweet when they met in the coffee shop down the street. She'd laugh at his jokes and call him Ronnie Pooh.

"Don't look at me like that. You love me."

"It wasn't love stupid. I was drunk. We were both drunk. You seemed to expect it and I felt sorry for you. I wish I'd never called you. I wouldn't have but all the other calls went to voicemail."

"But you did call me. You always call me when you're feeling down or need my help. I like helping you. I like being with you."

She pushed him away and got to the door without falling, then turned to look back at him with an ugly scowl on her once pretty face, "It was a pity fuck, you, dumb shit. And when I woke up the next morning, I thought I was going to puke when I realized you weren't Dave. Don't you get it, asshole?"

He let her go and watched her run out the door. At two in the morning he woke to the sound of his doorbell's buzz. He staggered to his feet and kicked the empty bottles of wine out of his way. When he opened the door, she was standing on the threshold weaving back and forth. Her hair had fallen out of its French knot, her lipstick was smeared as if someone had been kissing her. Evidently, she was in the mood to puke again. That didn't happen.

Ronnie Marchbello sank onto the couch and wiped his brow with a trembling hand. With a grimace he looked at the blood under his fingernails, then down at the woman he loved sprawled on his imitation bear-skin rug, her red dress against the synthetic fur looked like a pool of blood in a snowbank.

Holy Shit.

Fuck a Duck.

7…6…5

The distant throb of a car's motor startled Ronnie just as he was about to unlock the trunk of his Cadillac. He glanced over his shoulder. A van was climbing the winding hill road to the new construction site. The beam of the van's headlights bit through the dark. He stepped away from his car wondering frantically what to do. Had someone seen him carry the body from his back door to the alley? No. No. He'd been careful.

With the wind blowing a cold draft of air down his coat collar, he waited, hands thrust in his pockets, shivering and miserable. The familiar van pulled into the parking lot near the blue dumpster. He walked around the van past the glare of its headlights and glanced at the driver sitting inside watching him. He'd expected to see Bill Morris, but it was Millie Morris at the wheel of the Marchbello Construction Van.

She rolled down the window and he stepped up to the door. "What the hell are you doing here, Ronnie?" she demanded as if he were trespassing. "You're supposed to be bidding a new job in Sun Valley."

"I did that yesterday, Aunt Millie. What the hell are you doing here? It's four in the morning."

"Bill's sick. I came to drop off the van because your Dad called to tell me he needs the van for this new job."

He didn't believe her. "How are you getting home?"

"Dillon will be along soon. He'll be laying the new floor today."

"No, he won't. I told Dad I'd do it so that Dillon could go to Sun Valley with the surveyor."

She thrust the door open with such force, Ronnie sprang back before the door hit him in the chest. "The hell you are. You go on home and tell Dillon to come up here after breakfast. Laying concrete is for the experts not paper shufflers."

"I've done it a hundred times!"

"You're not the man to do this job, Ronald Marchbello. You've screwed up too many jobs in the past. Leave it to the experts."

"Screw you, Aunt Millie. I'm the Vice President at Marchbello and I'll do what ever the hell I want."

"We'll see about that boy. I'm going to call my brother and get this straightened out."

"Too late. Dad's already on the road by this time. He and Mom are going to see Grandma."

"You've got it all figured out, don't you? You gonna do this on your own, while nobody's watching. Think they won't notice once the concrete's cured and it's too late to fix it? Well, I got a vested interest in this company too, Ronald Marchbello, and I won't let you screw this one up."

"Damned it, Aunt Millie, just go home. I don't need the van today. Just let me do my job."

"Bullshit. I don't take orders from you. I'm staying right here."

He grabbed for her arm thinking he'd shove her back in the van. She jerked her arm out of his hold and he nearly fell on his face. She was a big woman, as tall as his father and just as strong. She'd worked for Marchbello Construction since the age of fourteen. There wasn't anything she hadn't done, from laying concrete to roofing.

He stepped back and tried to think. Millie watched him out of the corner of her eye and the look she gave him should have dropped him on the spot. He had an hour tops to lay the body out and start pouring the concrete. Damned Aunt Millie to hell. Bossy bitch.

"Alright. I suppose I'll need help with this. Why don't you go get Uncle Bill and he can help me?"

While they'd been arguing, the gray light of dawn crept over the horizon. On the other side of the valley a spark of gold lit the tip of the Sawtooth Mountains. Soon the light would sweep across the meadow turning it gold. Ronnie edged closer to Millie. Millie's usually ruddy cheeks were pale and drawn. "I told you. Bill is sick." She looked kind of sick herself. "He can't help you. And besides, he wouldn't let you so much as pick up a shovel. So, go home and call Dillon, tell him I'm at the site and preparing to pour in an hour."

"No. I'm doing this job. You go home and take care of Uncle Bill."

"Rat's Big Fat Ass if you are," she said, lifting her arm and swinging it back as if prepared to smack him across the face. He grabbed her wrist with both hands and squeezed.

"You may be used to beating on Dillon, but you'd better watch it, old lady. I don't take shit from you or any bitch."

She dropped her arm and staggered back, "How dare you! I never hit my Dillon, never."

The door of the cement truck opened with a shrill squeal startling them both. "That's right, Ronnie boy. You watch your mouth around my Momma," Dillon said between clenched teeth. Ronnie stepped back nervously as Dillon marched toward him.

"What the hell are you doing here? You're supposed to be meeting the surveyor."

"I had business to take care of first."

Ronnie noticed the mud on Dillon's boots and the shovel laying in the dirt near the hole. "You been working already?"

"Forgot my tool belt yesterday. Came to get it before you started pouring. Knowing you, you'd never have noticed."

Ronnie walked over to the hole and looked down. One small corner of the hard-packed dirt looked as if it had recently been dug up. "Why did you bury your tool belt, Dillon?"

"Shut your face, Ronnie or I'll shut it for you."

Ronnie spied Dillon's bike parked near the trees below the drive. There was a briefcase strapped to the back of the bike. The briefcase looked like one his father owned. What was Dillon doing with a fancy briefcase, anyway? Suspicious, Ronnie didn't wait to ask useless questions, but made a dash for the bike.

He heard the pounding of heavy feet right behind him. He pulled the briefcase off the bike, tucked it under his arm like a football and ran with his heart in his throat to the safety of his car. Once inside the car with the doors locked, he opened the briefcase. The car began to rock madly.

Dillon pounded on the roof, then the trunk, and bellowed like a mad bull in heat, "You, asshole. I'm gonna break your balls, you little wimp." Ronnie gasped at the contents in the briefcase. When Ronnie's trunk flew up from the force of Dillon's blows, Ronnie threw the briefcase onto the seat beside him. The zippered plastic bags were full of pot, powder, and pills. The rocking of the car sent a few bags tumbling to the floor. Ronnie fumbled at his car door trying to get it open. The rocking stopped.

He heard Aunt Millie screaming, "No, Dillon. Wait."

Ronnie looked out the window. Dillon was inside the Marchbello Van. His Aunt Millie's arms were wrapped around Dillon's legs in a feeble attempt to pull him out of the van. Ronnie thought it was best to get the hell out while he still had a chance. The engine purred to life. He pressed down on the gas pedal, spun the steering wheel and backed out of the drive. A body landed on the trunk. Ronnie glanced in his rearview mirror.

Dillon glared through the back windshield at his cousin, a hammer clutched in his fist. Ronnie spun the wheel back and forth trying to knock his cousin off the Cadillac. Millie chased after them hopping and screeching, loose hair sprouting from her bun like writhing snakes. No one was paying attention to the vehicle hugging the curve of the road climbing the hill fast.

4...3...2

"Before Christmas, this will be our new home, boys," Clifford Judge announced proudly, glancing in the back of his open bed truck at his three favorite Rottweilers. Back to the wild, Judge thought with satisfaction, back to the way life used to be, justice meant something then. Judge rounded the curve and the two vehicles collided.

1

Before impact Ronnie had a moment's regret – his seat belt. Millie heard metal strike metal and the sound echoing from mountain top to mountain top. Then she realized it was raining Rottweilers. She threw herself to the ground.

Ronnie lay on his back on something solid blood dripping into his eyes. He looked up and saw a Rottweiler sail over him and out of sight. The dog passed the sun and the sun winked. Ronnie tried to get up, the fingers of his right hand meeting the rough surface of a walrus rock. His body refused to obey. From the waist down he could feel nothing. He lay helpless watching as Aunt Millie ran past him screeching.

Judge saw the head lying on the seat next to him, brown eyes open and staring. Judge threw himself out of the cab. When he got to his feet, from the corner of his eye, he thought he saw the man's legs sticking out of his windshield. A crazy woman ran up to his truck and began to stroke the legs, babbling and whining, "Dillon? Baby? Speak to me."

Dazed, Judge searched for his crew. He saw a man on the other side of the road. He was draped over a walrus rock like a discarded Ken doll in an Armani suit. When Clifford Judge couldn't see his crew, he whistled. No one came. Discouraged, Judge clutched his broken arm and walked around the car searching the ridge above, while the mad woman bellowed in his ear then took off running down the road toward the valley.

Did she think she'd get to the police before him? He pulled out his cellphone turning his back on her. The road to his new home was a scene of carnage. He could smell blood everywhere, from the blood dripping down his face to the poor asshole in his windshield to the other poor asshole cooking over the walrus rock in the heat of the rising sun.

When the air quickened, Judge skidded to a stop dropping his phone. There was something off here. It was his last sane thought. Judge and Millie turned to look up at the ridge above the carnage. Three shadows stepped forward into the light. The crew spotted the wreckage below. As if they'd spotted rabbits, they raced down the hill. The sun rose to greet them, turning their black coats to blue, their eyes to red slits, their fangs to pearls. Judge, Ronnie and Millie had no time to pray, no time to be forgiven.

The cleanup crew had arrived.

Ruth Crawford paused in her writing with her best pen poised. A sound made her freeze afraid to look over her shoulder. She waited, hardly breathing. When she saw the cat slip inside the room and make for the couch, she relaxed. Shad must still be asleep in the next room. From the light of a newly emerging dawn, Ruth pulled her letter closer as if protecting its contents from prying eyes. There were no prying eyes in the house this early, just the birds in their cage and the tom cat sleeping on the armrest of the couch.

She set her pen to paper once more. She wrote: Yes, the reunion is on my birthday again this year. Samuel thinks that way nobody will quarrel. Don't be getting yourself all pickled over me. I'm still able. Samuel fixed up a steel bar in the bathroom so when grandpa climbs in the tub he won't fall and crack his head. He made me a new medicine cabinet too. Now grandpa's blood pressure medicines are in one place.

From the next room, she heard Shad turn over followed by a strangled clearing of the throat. She froze. Under her breath she commanded, "Go back to sleep. Go on; just five more minutes." With a sense of urgency, she finished her letter to Itty Bit no longer concerned about grammar, spelling, or legibility. *Angel brought over another greasy apple pie and when she left, I gave it to the pigs. I miss you so much. Love and kisses, Grandma.*

Ruth hoped that the image of Shad's sister pushing another one of her concoctions onto the family and the pigs receiving the fruits of her charity would bring a genuine smile to her granddaughter's normally enigmatic countenance.

Ruth loved discovering new words. Months ago, while she had been crossing the campus green clutching her library books, she had overheard one of the professors talking to a student and he had used a fascinating word, a word she had never heard before – enigmatic. She had repeated the word over and over inside her head so as not to forget and during a private moment searched through her personal dictionary.

It had been frustrating. She had tried under ineggmatic first. It had taken several days pouring over the dictionary until she thought she had the right word. Just to be sure, on her return to the library the following week, she had asked the librarian for help. And now because of all the fuss over that word, she would never forget it.

Yes. Itty Bit could be enigmatic, more so than any other person Ruth had ever met in her lifetime. Ruth would have liked to have been enigmatic. Maybe she was. At this very moment she could be anything she wished.

The house was quiet now, Shad having rolled onto his back and fallen asleep once again. It was just her and the animals, the ticking of the clock and the dripping of the faucet. Before leaving the house, Ruth glanced at herself in a small mirror by the door and tried to look enigmatic. The attempt made her laugh.

On Ruth's return from handing her letter to the postman and retrieving the household mail, she paused to examine her house. She thought about her house in relation to the larger world. She thought about the map, the one in Samuel's glove compartment that showed Boaz, Alabama in the north east corner, not too far from Gadsden, and closer to Rome, Georgia than Birmingham. The map could not begin to describe Boaz: chilly in the morning, hot by noon, homemade ice cream, lightning bugs, a distant second cousin of a town, and as solemn as a funeral procession.

Ruth had lived in Boaz most of her adult life. Having never left, she no longer paid much attention to the fact that her house stood last on the left-hand side of a dead-end street or that some folks might mistake the property beyond the house for an abandoned lot. She could barely remember when the house had been brand new. The peeling paint had long since dropped off and been sucked down into the red soil.

It was impossible to see the house with fresh eyes. Forty years of acquaintance could not be erased overnight. Her house looked as it had always looked. The few blue flakes still clinging to the house, she'd been told by the grandchildren, looked real pretty. Years ago, they'd offered to go into town and get the paint and paint the whole house in one summer. Wouldn't Grandpa Shad be tickled, they'd said?

She wouldn't know. Even if he liked the idea, where would they find the money? The bits of brilliant blue, way up high where the children and animals couldn't get to them, protected by a dispirited roof and clinging to the past, were like everything else around these parts; they were a reminder of an old pain best left to rot.

What with her windows open and her white curtains motionless and the porch in-between with its sagging roof, all these facts made her think of age, of an old woman with her eyes rolled back in her head, the whites the only vision left to her. The porch roof was the old woman's stroke smile.

The letters and junk mail crackled as Ruth held them tight to her chest. With each step she made toward the porch, she could feel her legs sting and burn, as if firecrackers had been thrown down in her path. Ruth opened the screen door and stepped into the dark parlor. Shad's pile of Reader's Digest subscriptions had spilled off the couch and onto the rag rug under the coffee table. She'd spent the entire winter of 1943 choosing castoffs from the family's pile of old clothes making the rag rug. It had kept her busy instead of fretting about her boy fighting in France.

Ruth missed library days, missed walking to Snead State Community College library and standing by the fiction section collecting titles. Mostly, she missed the anticipation of sitting down to read a new book. If her son Samuel took her to the library, he always complained about how much time she took looking for a good read. Her favorite books were about faraway places in Canada or Europe or China. Only last year, she'd read *The Good Earth*. Those little yellow people weren't much different from her kind of folks.

Shad was waiting for her at the head of the kitchen table. Ruth put the mail down in front of his plate, knowing that her own letter from Itty Bit rested safe and secure in her dress pocket. She sat down at her usual place, the opposite end of the table near the window. Shad ate his breakfast.

From the open window a breeze carried the smells of spring into the room. Ruth breathed in deep the reminders of life: grass growing in the field, Shad's old privy still smelling of lye, the early blooming purple and white lilacs, a courageous red carnation. She could see her rhododendron near the clothesline. She could hear a yellowhammer knocking his way through one of the house shingles and the rustle of sumac leaves as the tom prowled under the bush.

Ruth had tried to kill the sumac. The sumac made your skin burn and itch. The sumac refused to die. In the distance, Ruth could see Samuel's bull standing under the southern red oak, separated from the cows today.

She interrupted her breakfast to pour her husband Shad a cup of coffee and in between the time of moving to the stove and returning with the coffee pot, Shad had gobbled down her cornbread. She filled his cup and returned to her seat. Her poached eggs and steak were cold. Shad had tried to fix the radio, but after breaking off the knob, he and she had had to suffer through Gadsden's choice of popular tunes. Ruth heard some male singing, "rolling, rolling, rolling down the river" and tried to figure out what the initials CCR stood for.

Shad stopped chewing. The unnatural silence in the room made Shad and Ruth turn to stare at the radio. They relaxed when a voice announced breaking news. Ruth thought the news might have something to do with flooding in the Mississippi Delta or maybe rainstorms coming their way from the Gulf of Mexico. Ruth recognized a name and turned her head to hear the better. The announcer was talking about Martin Luther King Junior, about an assassination in Memphis, Tennessee.

Shad threw down his fork, jumped up from his chair, and started dancing a jig around the kitchen. His boots stomped on the few stupid cockroaches still scuttling about in the dark corners of the room. Most of the roaches fled when they entered the room, or the light hit the floor; others were more determined. On this day, two of them, the slower moving ones, ended up as smears on the bottom of Shad's boots.

"Hallelujah! That bastard is finally dead and gone. Dead and gone," he shouted, so ecstatic he did not notice Ruth sitting with her head down and her hands folded in her lap. Ruth disbelieved the news. There had been a mistake. His joy at this man's death sickened her beyond measure.

Itty Bit's letter was still in her pocket reminding her of people who would be devastated by the poor man's death. She got up from her seat on shaky legs and switched off the radio. Itty Bit had mentioned once that Dr. King was a sensible man, a good, kind man. She forced the tears back. In private. She'd weep in private. Ruth looked at Shad acting like he'd won a prize, jumping about the room like an idjit. She'll have to clean his boots with a stick or make him do it.

Then she noticed a roach on the top of the table heading for her plate. Ruth used her broom and swept the roach onto the floor. The hairs on her neck stiffened in disgust. She felt an urgent need to rinse the plates under the faucet before dumping them in hot soapy water.

Shad, now calm, without a word reached for his shotgun. With a bang of the screen door he left her in the gloomy kitchen. In his wake, blessed peace descended. She heard him shuffle across the porch. She knew he was nearly to the steps when one of the boards grumbled. He took the steps one at a time just like the babies had taken them. She heard him whack the gate with the toe of his boot and call out to Samuel, his voice sounding more like a hound dog with a cold than a man.

She remembered the first time he'd spoken to her back in 1921. She'd just turned fifteen and he'd come home a sailor having traveled all over the world. His voice used to make the nerves along her scalp tingle. Nowadays, the only thing that made her scalp tingle was coffee.

Ruth sipped her coffee. It tasted like overcooked steak.

Once he was gone, Ruth could hear the kitchen noises – a hundred tiny feet exploring the floor and the countertop, water dripping from the tap, Amos and Andy in their cage singing to each other. She blamed the oak tree for her dark kitchen. It hadn't been so when she was a new bride. Through the kitchen window, she watched as Shad made his way across the field to Samuel's house.

The field needed mowing; Shad's pants needed to be taken in around the hips again too. She watched him hold up his pants with one hand and with the other carry his shotgun. She shouted through the open window, "Buy yourself a frigging belt, Shadow Crawford. You're gonna shoot your fool head off," then began to cough and didn't stop coughing until she drank her glass of water. He ignored her as usual, didn't even look back to see why she was coughing.

Ruth dried the last glass, wiped her hands on her apron, and with a stubby pencil wrote down *mow field* and *sew up cords* on the roll of paper hanging from the wooden box Samuel had made her in the fifth grade. Ruth returned to the window in time to see her husband bang on Samuel's front door with the butt of his rifle. Samuel opened the door wearing nothing but his underwear. Shad waved his rifle in the air and before entering the house let off a few rounds. Samuel backed away and rubbed the sleep out of his eyes.

If Samuel's elder brother Jeremiah had survived, he would have taken Shad's rifle away from him and thrashed him good. Ruth had been so proud of Jeremiah in his uniform. He had looked so tall and handsome. If Ruth had had the money, she would have gone to that place the soldier had told her about, that place called Saint-Lō, even if she had to take two planes and a train to go. And when she got there, she would see for herself where her son had died. The marine said Jeremiah had died without feeling anything. She'd said to that soldier, "How'd you know? You got some special sense that knows how other folks feel when they die?"

Ruth still had Itty Bit, Itty Bit looked a lot like her daddy Jeremiah, same reddish-brown hair and hazel eyes. And like her daddy, Itty Bit had left Boaz young and only came back to say good-bye again. "Come with me Grandma, come to Memphis with me and march," Itty Bit had said.

"Itty Bit, your grandpa would never let me go," Ruth had told her. "And besides politics makes me nervous. Let people be I say. Things'll work out."

"Don't call me Itty Bit any more Grandma. I don't like it. I never liked it. Call me by my name, my real name."

"You know how I feel about living up to a name," Ruth said.

"But Esther was the queen of Persia. That's something worth living up to."

"But she lived a lie. She lived in fear. That's no life."

"In the end she told the truth and saved her people."

Ruth watched Itty Bit's hazel eyes storing memories. It had been just the two of them in the room saying their good-byes. Itty Bit had ironed her hair straight. It looked like dark auburn hay. She wore baggy blue jeans and some sort of a blouse. She looked like a temperamental ten-year-old dressed in someone else's clothes. She would never get any bigger the doctor had said.

Ruth imagined Itty Bit marching with all those people and getting herself lost among the forest of bodies, maybe, getting herself trampled to death. Ruth glanced at the picture of Shad standing by his ship in his white sailor's uniform between two average sized sailors. He looked like a child standing between two adults. Shad had survived the navy. Itty Bit would survive university and all the fiery speeches and pushy people.

Shortly after the fight with her grandfather Itty Bit left Boaz for good. Shad had stormed out of the house that night and only come home from his important poker game the next day. All he could say to her was, "You screwed up their minds Ruth, screwed 'um up with your fancy notions from dumb books. We live here in Boaz. Not some tow-pee-a." Her husband could be as mean as a badger when he was feeling sorry for himself.

"UTOPIA. It's spelled u t o p i a."

"I know Utopia, Miss Educated. Utopia is some place you go AFTER you are dead."

Ruth left the dishes to soak, wiped her hands on her apron and stepped outside. She might have five or ten minutes just to sit and do nothing. She might have all morning. She sat on the porch swing and counted what she'd done so far this morning and what she wanted to do before bedtime. Ruth heard the ghost of Shad's voice tickling her ear. His young voice made her think of whiskey and smoke and dancing to a saxophone slow with hips rubbing, "Ruth Nicole Crawford. My Nikki."

In the distance, Ruth thought she saw Laurel running across the pasture toward her, running with her cotton dress flapping about her stocky legs. Laurel had set her hair free from its usual braid, the thick curly strands as black as raspberries and flying, this way and that, reminding Ruth of a picture she'd seen of Medusa. No longer amused, Ruth saw her and thought how Laurel seemed all exposed, exposed to the wind and the pasture and the eyes of strangers.

Ruth closed her eyes and opened them again. In the pasture, Samuel's heifers were nursing their calves. The tom cat, curled in an ebony ball, slept on the seat of Samuel's tractor with the sun turning his coat blue. A wren swooped down and rested for a moment on the barbed wire fence.

The reunion would be on Sunday. There would be complaints if the kids didn't get to go to Little River Canyon and spend the day near the falls and have their picnic and swim in the river. Shad would warn the little ones to be extra careful cause of the near drowning and he'd look to Ruth to tell the story. The little ones would eat ice cream and apple pie and listen and applaud.

This year Ruth wanted to go somewhere else. She wanted to see the Gulf of Mexico before she died. Samuel might take her. No. Samuel would not. Samuel would do what his daddy wanted him to do. Joshua would arrive in his new car from Baton Rouge. Opal and Ruby would surely come. Opal in Atlanta, just a hop and a skip away would bring her hubby Oxley and Oxley would get Shad all riled up and ready for mischief. Ruby in Montgomery would cart all those damn kids and all her damn laundry home and expect her mother to take care of the lot.

The reunion would be at the pool. Shad would bring up the near drowning and look to Ruth to tell the story. Ruth thought the cat might be interested in the story. The tom cat's ears twitched as she began to speak, "It was the summer of 1932 and Shad and me and your parents were swimming in Little River Canyon. We had a picnic by the shore. Your parents were about your age. They were running through the trees, over rocks, in the stream, everywhere. Jeremiah found a real pretty spot by a rocky ledge. The water tumbles off that ledge down, down, into a deep, deep, pool, a pool so deep nobody has ever touched bottom."

Ruth remembered that day. The children had been chattering as they climbed up from the pool, all skinny, nothing but white, wet, shivering popsicles waiting for their turn to jump off. She saw Laurel, eight years old again, poised on the ledge prepared to jump and her daddy waiting below to help her if she took fright. She saw Laurel, all child, naïve and foolish and courageously dumb, throw up her arms and jump off screaming with joy, her screams bouncing off rocks and trees, bouncing down the river.

Ruth remembered the colored boys waiting for their turn to jump. The little one, no more than five or six, with his huge black eyes and bowed legs had jumped off the ledge feet first with his eyes open. Her boys were at the bottom hoping to catch him before he tumbled down the river. He did not pop up like the others. Shad dove into the pool and Ruth counted under her breath.

No one spoke. The reflection of the sun's light on the water burned her eyes. A thought crept up on her unawares; it began with a poke at the back of her neck and crawled its way like a garden snake over her scalp. The thought created nausea in her stomach and excitement along her spine. And then the dread returned, and her forehead began to ache with worry. She was instantly ashamed.

Then she saw Shad's black hair, then his face, the forehead, nose, and cheeks red from a new sun, the rest of him golden pecan. Shad towed the boy toward the bank. While the spectators played statues, Shad pumped water out of the boy's lungs. When the colored boy gasped for air and began coughing, Shad tossed back a strand of wet hair from his brow and smiled in triumph. Laurel had been on the ledge watching. Laurel's voice had carried clear to Huntsville, "That's my Daddy. You all know my Daddy."

Laurel's voice in Ruth's head brought on the chest pains. She couldn't stand the pain, couldn't catch a breath. Ruth struggled to get herself off the swing. She scooted forward using the strength in one shaky arm to lift herself up. Once she was standing, she set one swollen foot in front of the other. She took the stairs one at a time. She fought the uneven porch planks. The old boards groaned.

Once inside, she made her way to the laundry room and stood by the wringer washing machine. She used a pair of Shad's underwear to slap the dirt and bugs off the mesh screen, then peered out the window. Shad must have invited himself into Samuel's house for a second breakfast. The fingers of her right hand refused to close. She leaned against the door frame for a moment her face hot and sweaty.

Firecrackers shot up her arm. Laurel's old dress had gotten too big for Ruth. Through the gap in her dress, Ruth could see her bra and stomach. She watched the bead of sweat slide down between her breasts. Like a tear, the droplet continued to fall until it rested on her belly.

Ruth made her way to the bedroom and lay down on the bed. Martin Luther King Junior had died. She did not know him. She knew of him though – through the eyes of her granddaughter. Itty Bit had written to her about him and about the people marching arm and arm. Itty Bit had made everything seem so real, more real than the news. After Ruth read Itty Bit's letter, she burned her granddaughter's words and the envelope, then mixed the ashes in with the soil around the few white carnations still alive in her garden. She stayed down on her hands and knees and smelled the earth and the growing plants.

Shad had seen her sniffing the ground and said, "You look like one of the cats. Why don't you pick a few of those damned things and smell um proper?"

"I like them in the ground alive and growing," she told him.

If Shad came home and found her on the bed in the middle of the day, he'd fuss over her. Ruth made herself get up. But when her feet touched the floor, her right leg turned to salt. She fell and hit her head on the edge of the night table. The lamp, her most prized possession, with its pearl colored globe, shattered into three pieces. Ruth lay where she had fallen with her cheek pressed against the floorboard and blood as a pillow. The tongue and groove oak boards hadn't been stained or sealed in years.

The wood drank in her blood as greedy as a suckling newborn. She smelled the iron and was amazed at the peace inside herself, amazed at her calm acceptance of blood disfiguring her floor, blood marking this spot as if it had been scorched. She must have cracked herself a good one, cracked open her skull most likely. Her heart recovered its rhythm, but her head still throbbed. Ruth lay on the floor, not wanting to get up. From this new perspective, she could see something under the bed. She sneezed.

The something under the bed reminded her of a small shiny black coffin, a child's coffin enshrined in dust bunnies and cobwebs. Then she recognized it – her old trunk. Her old dresses were inside the trunk. Jeremiah had been the first to find it. He pestered Ruth until she gave in and put on one of her old dresses. The dress she chose had been worn only once, back when she and Shad had been courting. It looked best on women with narrow hips and breasts the size of flapjacks. She'd worn the dress for the first time Shad took her to a speakeasy, the first time she'd ever sipped whiskey and saw women smoking cigars.

After eight years and five children, the dress fit tight across her chest and hips and hung in apology two inches above her knees. As she showed off the dress, holding her arms up and spinning around and dancing for them, Jeremiah, then seven years old, rolled on the bed and clutched his stomach laughing in short barks like his daddy. Laurel had been three and transfixed by the dress. Laurel's eyes had glistened drunk in the half light, drunk with all the beads and the colors whirling by her face. She'd grabbed hold of Ruth's hem and followed Ruth around the room, stroking the beads like they had been the ears of a cat.

The last time Laurel wore the bead dress she'd been fourteen. All the details of that ugly year came back to Ruth with a force as mindless and furious as the waters of the Little Canyon: the year Jeremiah came inside with the welt of his father's hand on his bare chest and Ruth followed him out to the road and watched him walk away without remembering her, walk away as if he were maneuvering through a mine field. It was that year Shad gave up on the boys and let them run wild. It was that year the girls got his full attention.

Ruth had seen her from the kitchen window that day, had seen Laurel cut across the field jumping over tall grass and wildflowers, running with her braid undone and her dress soaked with sweat. Ruth remembered the way the sun burned down on Laurel's head. Ruth saw Laurel and the field and Shad, and the house bleached of color. Ruth could hear someone working the blades of a push lawnmower, stopping and starting, and cussing in-between.

All morning, the house had been without color. Samuel and his friends had gone to watch the baseball game at Paradise Park. There had been no one stomping through the rooms; no one slamming doors; no one begging for something to eat, just Ruth and Shad waiting. And there she was moving from one window to the next hoping she'd be the first to see Laurel. And all morning, Shad had been out on the back porch sitting on the step drinking whiskey and soda trying to kill himself some squirrels.

Ruth knew if she went out on the porch one more time, Shad would leave and go find the boy and maybe shoot him instead of the squirrels. Ruth had been at the kitchen window when she spied Laurel crossing the pasture headed for home. Why? Why now? Laurel had stopped at the gate to catch her breath. Ruth remembered the way Laurel rested her forehead in the pillow of her arms. Ruth saw again the dimples in Laurel's elbows, the sunburned arms, the bangs soaked with sweat. They were children. They were just children. They didn't know no better.

Shad's shout scared the birds off the fence. Laurel lifted her head and looked at her daddy with old eyes. Ruth remembered leaving the kitchen and seeing Shad yank his belt off his hips. Ruth remembered thinking, Laurel will survive, all the boys had survived. Not once did she open her mouth, not once. She just.

She remembered finding herself standing a block away from her house with her arms wrapped around her waist, as if she needed her arms to hold herself together. She recognized Mrs. Anderson's hydrangea bush. Mrs. Anderson liked her flowers one color – pink. Then Ruth heard Laurel scream. She didn't want to remember anymore. But like usual the memories refused to die.

Ruth still prone on her bedroom floor stared at her old trunk. Whenever she replayed that day, she imagined herself going out to the woodshed and saying something, anything, she imagined herself a different person. Whenever she replayed that day, she tried to make herself turn around and go back to the house. She did none of those things.

Mrs. Armstrong had given Ruth a damp washcloth to wipe away the blood from her chin. She'd bitten right through her lip. Sometimes Ruth dreamt herself five extra minutes. Laurel would be down at Paradise Park and Ruth would go to her and warn her and they would walk to the library and sit under the arbor on the bench and watch the grass grow. In all her dreaming over the years Ruth never imagined herself taking the belt away. Why? Why can't she dream herself brave?

From far away, Ruth heard Samuel and Shad enter the kitchen. Samuel's weight and his heavy boots made the floorboards shake. Ruth's body rocked up and down, keeping time with Samuel's rhythm. Samuel called out to her. She tried to get up, but her right side refused to wake up. Shad opened the ice box. She heard the satisfying hiss as he pulled back the tab and drank the soda, knowing how he liked to throw back his head and let the liquid slide down his throat. She heard him slam the Westinghouse door so hard the shock rattled the bottles inside. The last thing she did was sigh in annoyance.

Ruth woke in the hospital bed. She'd never been in a hospital before. Maybe this is a kind of escape, only further than the bus station. At the bus station, people showed up and cried and said they were sorry and begged you to come home. At the bus station, a child sat alone with a ticket to Atlanta. It was supposed to be temporary, just for the summer and she would return for school. It was never meant to be forever. It was never meant to be good-bye. Ruth had been thinking about that day for so many years, it was only now she knew – she knew for sure that she might as well have been at her child's funeral.

It didn't matter.

Laurel was alive somewhere, all grown up, maybe with a family of her own. It didn't matter that she had grandchildren somewhere Ruth would never know. To never see her child again, never hear from her, never know if she was safe or happy – that constant ache every night knowing another day had passed in silence, yes, her daughter might as well be dead. And thinking it different wouldn't make the grieving any less painful.

She used her useful arm and covered her mouth with the extra hospital pillow so as not to wake the patient in the next bed, until the nurses got scared and the doctor came. He shot her up with something which was supposed to give her some peace. There was no peace. There would never be peace or most especially important – forgiveness. She wanted to be forgiven. If she could find Laurel and say her piece maybe the firecrackers inside would stop.

They put her on a different floor. She observed the wariness in the eyes of the nurses and didn't care. They made her do silly tasks as if she were a child again. She did what she was told; she'd been raised to do what she was told. And then there came a day when they returned her to her old room.

At the hospital people visit for a spell and leave you in peace. Ruth likes the idea of visiting hours. Every home should have visiting hours. Samuel sits beside Ruth's bed and she hears him say, "Mom. Mom. I hope you can hear me. I got to tell you about Dad. He's gone Mom. The doctor said nobody's to blame."

Ruth – in-between – smiles her stroke smile. She's nearly home. She stands in front of the hydrangea bush and stares at the pink flowers. She will plant a blue hydrangea by the dead sumac. She hears Laurel shout, "That's my Daddy. You all know my Daddy." Ruth turns and runs toward the house convinced Laurel is waiting for her on the porch.

On a fine July morning, Ruth Crawford sits on the steps of her house with her trunk at her feet and waits for Itty Bit to come fetch her. Along the edge of the fence, the red oak shades the pasture. The bull is gone. Samuel had to sell him to pay for the hospital visit and the funeral.

Ruth has her trunk packed with new clothes, a new pair of black pumps, and a new book. The book's pages are crisp and white, the ink bold and black. Joshua is back home in Baton Rouge and still grumbling cause nobody wants to sue the soda company. Everybody is upset that the reunion has been postponed once again. Ruth will read her new book on the beach. She will stare out at the clear waters of the Gulf of Mexico and dream that Shad gets himself a better master.

An hour later, Itty Bit arrives driving a Volkswagen bus the color of an aphid with stickers and spray paint wallpapering the chrome fenders, the windows, the doors, even the roof. Itty Bit refuses to answer to her old nickname. Ruth sits in Esther's Volkswagen mortified; what will her neighbors think of her sitting in such a contraption?

Once they reach the edge of town, Ruth leans back in her seat and unclenches her hands. Esther pulls over onto the shoulder of the road and winks at Ruth, "You just sit back and relax Grandma; I'll take good care of you."

Ruth looks out the passenger window. On the hill above her, she sees a child about two or three. His mama has cut a hole in a burlap sack for his head to slide through and two holes for his arms. He waddles up the hill, bare arms and legs the color of milk chocolate. He falls over in the grass and gets up holding something in his hand. He waves to her. She waves back.

THEM COCKEYED OPTIMISTS

Noticed the last few posts on my website have been filled with angst and suppressed rage. Don't want to end the month raging against the threat to our democracy. Must remember I once-upon-a-time had a sense of humor. I've never been good at remembering jokes. My humor is unintentional. Even in my writing I find spelling mistakes or grammatical mistakes which when reread are hilarious. I thought I'd reached the age by now when I would have become a little wiser and a little more dignified.

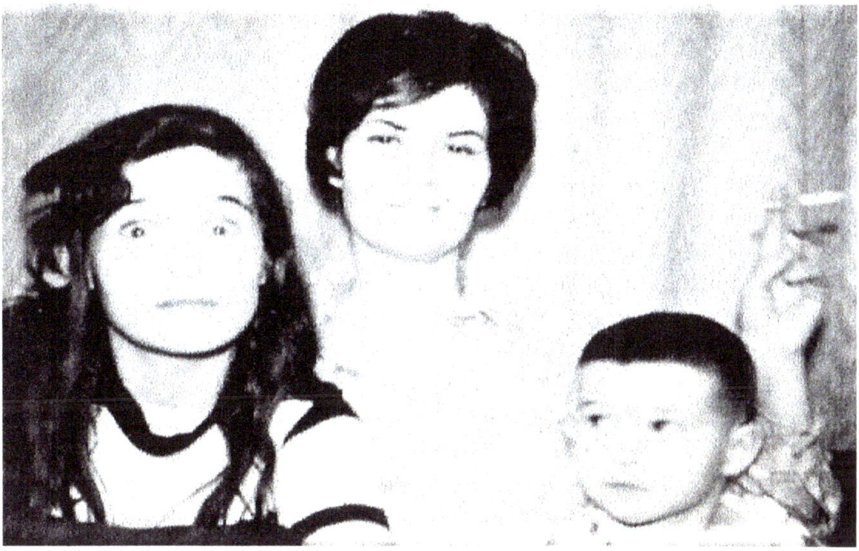

K McVere LLC © 2018

Nope.

I'm still the same kid I was when I was ten and the school bus driver asked, "Is anyone else a cockeyed optimist?" His question put the bus filled with children in a blinding panic. You could feel the bus fill with thick globules of test anxiety. Then he said, "Well, I am. I'm a cockeyed optimist and you should be too." None of us knew if we were cockeyed optimists or regular optimists or if maybe he was hinting some of us needed eyeglasses, but because I felt sorry for him, I said, "Me too. I'm one of those." I remember the kids laughed and the bus driver laughed, and all was right with the world again.

Over fifty years have gone by and I still blurt out stuff I wish I could take back. Like the time in my thirties when all the women in the office where I worked were sharing stories about their fathers, what their fathers did for a living and how much they loved their fathers. One of my coworkers said, “My father’s a lawyer.” Another woman told the group, “My father is a high school biology teacher.” And I piped up and said, “My father’s a bank robber.” They laughed and shook their heads, not a one believing me. But I was telling the truth. Honestly.

The man who adopted me, when I was barely a year old, happened to be a bank robber. Well, he wasn’t a bank robber when he adopted me. No. He started robbing banks a few years later. When they realized I wasn’t joking, they apologized for laughing. I’d laughed along with them because I just couldn't resist blurting out the truth. The opening had been too good to pass up. It was true my father had been a bank robber. He paid for his mistakes and when I was older returned to society and never robbed banks again.

I never really knew him because during my childhood he was in one prison or another. He eventually ended up in Leavenworth and we had a lovely two-year correspondence. His advice has stayed with me. And he had the neatest penmanship I’ve ever seen, from anyone, back then, and even today. He was also incredibly smart. Too bad he had to go to prison, he could have been anything: an architect, a map maker, even a hedge fund billionaire.

So, back when I was thirty, the women in the office, whenever they’d see me, would smile remembering my outburst as I proudly proclaimed, “My father’s a bank robber.” They didn’t seem to mind. They didn’t take the fact my father was a bank robber out on me. They could have, but I was lucky. They were a sweet bunch of ladies.

There are days, even now, when I slip back into my cockeyed optimist “me too” outbursts when I go into work and speak aloud thoughts better left unsaid. I do try to think before I speak, but sometimes I get so excited I forget to check the words through my inner editor. For example, the other day at work I showed up and while I’m punching in my identification number, I say to my coworkers in the back room, “I want to be disciplined.” Everyone in the backroom laughed and teased me making euphemistic suggestions about how I could be disciplined.

Because the people I work with are so much fun to be around, I joined in the laughter. Only at home in quiet reflection do I wish sometimes I could edit my thoughts before they reach my mouth. Maybe because I feel so comfortable with these folks, I just blurt out what’s on my mind in shorthand. When I mentioned disciplined, I meant that I wanted to write four hours a day on weekdays, finish a blog once a week and spend the rest of my time managing my social media platforms. To my way of thinking, if I were more disciplined, I might have finished the draft of April Fools by now.

Sadly, I'm not as disciplined as I used to be. Lately, I'm letting distractions get the best of me. Or maybe I'm just too ambitious? Maybe I've set unrealistic goals? Have I really? How many writers who work another job can edit three books in two years? Maybe more than I realize. Maybe none. I don't know for sure. I can only guess. One of my colleagues at work said in an off-hand manner, "I bet you always used to sit in the front of the classroom."

Yes.

As a freshman in college, I used to sit in the center row right up front. And yes, other freshman students used to tease me about being an overachiever.

Maybe I am.

But what has it got me? I have several college degrees and still struggle to pay the bills. When I was in college, I noticed how some students didn't even bother to come to class or speak up in class or finish their portfolios, but they managed to get their degrees. I bet they're doing just fine. I envy them their laidback sangfroid attitudes. Why can't I be more like them? Why am I so hard on myself all the time?

The answer was revealed to me last night, a sort of epiphany created by urgency. You see, the urgency was plugging my ears. I searched the house for earplugs. I tried them and they didn't cut out the noise. I ended up shredding an old dish towel and tried to stick the bits in my ears to shut out the noise. It didn't work. Then I gave in and just laid in bed and listened. The connection between my sympathy for the poor animal and pity for myself brought me to a eureka moment.

It took a hound dog's hysterical barking in the wee hours of the night for me to connect his despair at being separated from his beloved owner with my experience as a newborn. My mother told me the story of my birth. She said a priest took me out of her arms when I was a few hours old with the intention of sending me off to an orphanage. Since she was unwed at the time, and it was the 1950s, and I was born in a Catholic hospital, the priest believed he had the authority to decide my future.

Without consulting my mother or my grandpa he decided to give me to a nun so that I might be adopted by a good Catholic family and raised in a proper home. My mother and my grandpa when they found out went apeshit, made a scene in the hospital halls and the priest reluctantly brought me back. If they had complied with the priest's decision, my life might have been very different.

There were days in my teens when I wished I'd been adopted, but as a grandmother looking back, even remembering the bad times, I'm still grateful to have been raised by my mother. She was the kind

K McVere LLC © 2018

of woman who hated prejudice of any kind, who washed our mouths out with soap when we repeated racists words we heard at school. By her example I learned to love books, be brave and never give up.

And I believe the reason Grandpa Shorty went apeshit over my abduction was because I was born with red hair and he took this as an excellent sign that he and I shared the all-powerful Irish ancestry. Somehow, he'd gotten it into his head that his ancestry was inferior because he was so damned short. Since I had red hair, he decided his shortness was confirmation he was Irish.

Whatever his reasons were for insisting the priest return his granddaughter to the hospital room, I am grateful. Grandpa Shorty, your intervention allowed me to get to know three incredibly strong independent women: my mother, my grandmother, and my great-grandmother.

Therefore, after a sleepless night, I've decided that instead of beating myself up all the time, I need to factor in annoying interruptions as a reason I can't finish the draft of April Fools. I get them all the time - interruptions, the knocks on the door, a ubiquitous eager face leaning in hoping to sell me something: a political candidate I've never heard of, a wireless plan I don't want, or lawn care I don't need since I don't have a lawn. And then there are the nights when the neighborhood is on fire with dogs barking and people partying. After a few hours' sleep, I'm a zombie. All I want to do is eat a brain, not just any brain, the brain responsible for keeping me awake.

It's time to be a cockeyed optimist, for real, full time, no stops.

Between life's interruptions and my overachieving personality my cockeyed optimism is looking positively levelheaded, maybe even brilliant.

Just now I created an alarm on my cellphone – Cockeyed Optimist. The alarm will remind me: don't be so hard on yourself; don't be an overachiever; if you do, you might end up a success and success disciplines even the best of writers.

Sad, but true.

K McVere LLC © 2020
Father No. 5

www.ingramcontent.com/pod-product-compliance
Lightning Source LLC
Chambersburg PA
CBHW062023290426
44108CB00024B/2763
* 9 7 8 0 5 7 8 5 8 0 9 9 9 *